Mystic Masonry

Or the Symbols of Freemasonry and the Greater Mysteries of Antiquity

By J. D. Buck

Made a Master Mason, Battle Creek, Mich. September 27, 1864.
Made a Royal Arch Mason, Sandusky, Ohio. November 27, 1867.
Royal and Select Master, Sandusky, Ohio, 1868.
DeMolay Commandery, Republic, Ohio, 1869.
320 Scottish Rite, Northern Jurisdiction, May 1873.
330 Honorary, Scottish Rite, Northern Detroit, Michigan, September 1910.

PANTIANOS
CLASSICS

Published by Pantianos Classics

ISBN-13: 978-1-78987-471-6

First published in 1896

This reprint is derived from the third edition of 1911

MYSTIC

MASONRY

The Original Front Cover, 1911

Jirah Dewey Buck,

1838 – 1916.

Contents

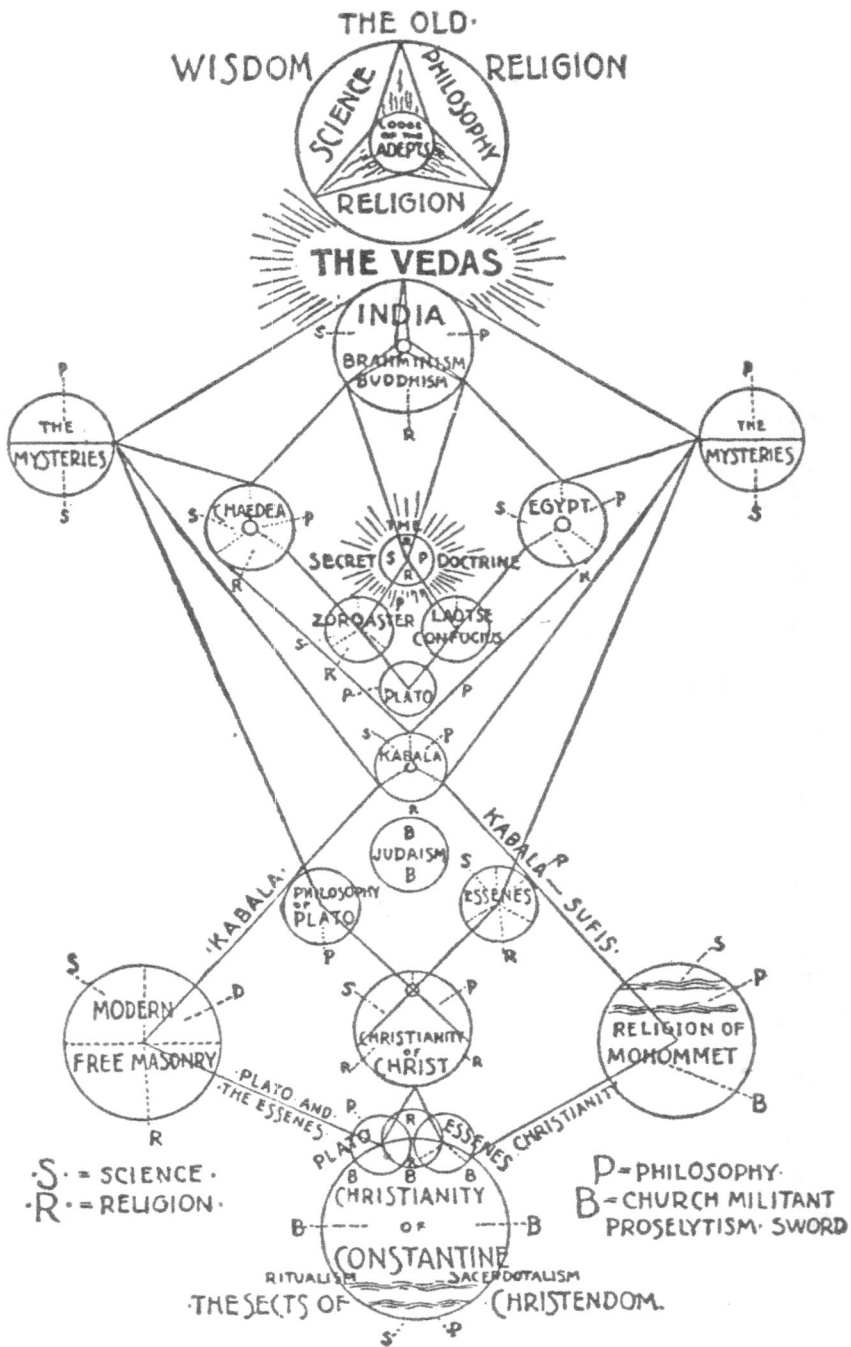

THE OLD·

WISDOM RELIGION

SCIENCE · PHILOSOPHY · RELIGION

LODGE OF THE ADEPTS

RELIGION

THE VEDAS

INDIA

BRAHMANISM BUDDHISM

THE MYSTERIES

THE MYSTERIES

CHALDEA

EGYPT

THE SECRET DOCTRINE

ZOROASTER

LAOTSE CONFUCIUS

PLATO

KABALA

JUDAISM

KABALA — SUFIS·

PHILOSOPHY OF PLATO

ESSENES

MODERN FREE MASONRY

CHRISTIANITY OF CHRIST

RELIGION OF MOHOMMET

·S· = SCIENCE·
·R· = RELIGION·

PLATO· AND·
THE ESSENES

PLATO

ESSENES CHRISTIANITY

CHRISTIANITY OF CONSTANTINE

P = PHILOSOPHY·
B = CHURCH MILITANT
PROSELYTISM· SWORD

RITUALISM SACERDOTALISM

·THE SECTS OF CHRISTENDOM·

FRONTISPIECE.

VI

Foreword to the Third Edition

The spirit of unrest is in the air. On the surface of things today, Commercialism most often and most loudly claims attention. Great combinations of capital and the massing of millions seem the order of the day. Within the body politic organization and cooperation is being tried on a scale never before recorded in the history of man, and economic problems are being tested in a way that cannot help adding immensely to the combined experience of mankind. What the final outcome may be, only the wisest could now say, and perhaps only the foolish would venture to predict.

But human nature is essentially a stable product, and can be relied on in any event. Deep in the heart of man lies the principle of justice and equity, and no abuse that selfishness and greed can devise can long have any permanency. We may be far from the universal reign of Brotherhood, but there is something deep down in the heart of man that continually strives toward it.

Potent as is all this commercial unrest and economic strife, other problems are equally up for solution. Using the term in its broadest sense, the Psychic problem keeps pace with the economic. Ethics and Economics are inseparable. The conduct of the individual, and the use of the resources of life and the distribution of wealth, always involve both ethics and economics; in short, constitute them.

Outside the churches and religious literature we hear less about religion nowadays. Indeed, many otherwise good people seem to think religion obsolete; a thing of the past; a survival — where, indeed, it is admitted to have survived at all — of the dark ages. No greater mistake could possibly be made. The surface problems may have changed; organizations may have broken up or disappeared, but the vital issues not only remain, but were never more in evidence than today. Nor can it be otherwise so long as the essential nature of man remains unchanged.

Only the imbecile or the degenerate can really ignore the religious element in his own nature if he tries. Just as inevitably as water seeks its level, and ultimately finds its way to the sea, does man *feel* after that Power — called by whatsoever name — whose divine ray makes him Man, and whose indwelling presence lifts him, at rare moments, beyond sordid self, and beckons his soul toward the higher, the larger, the better, as by the touch of wings. This is a universal experience, equally known to the savage and the civilized, and entirely independent of theologies or ecclesiasticism. Theologians in all ages have seized hold of this common human experience and formulated and endeavored to guide it, and have often exploited it, just as capitalists have dealt with economic problems in the resources of nature and the distribution of wealth.

This is, broadly speaking, the psychic problem, constituting the religious element in the life of man. It was never more manifest than it is today. This it is that now runs *pari passu* with commercialism; and while, as already said, it may make less noise, it is everywhere in evidence.

Every problem in the life of man, and every movement that affects society, is, in the last analysis, a psychic problem. One and all they concern the body and its environments incidentally, and the soul essentially.

The progress made in physical science in the last half century is so remarkable that it is difficult to find an adjective suitable with which to designate it. Hence the economic problems already referred to are necessarily to be revised.

While the psychic problems have come into equal prominence, no such organized results can be pointed out as in economic experiments. The race, as a whole, has been gathering facts and making experiments. The working hypothesis in psychology has seldom been suggested. At any rate, there is no large or general agreement as to any theorems. There seem to be no designs on the trestle-board, and the workmen, the legions, are in confusion.

The great majority of people, even among the educated and intelligent, will make haste to deny that this psychic theorem has ever been known to man. That it could ever have been discovered and then lost, or concealed, is to them preposterous; yet the whole of the traditions and symbolism of Masonry cluster around this *theorem,* this working hypothesis in the psychical life of man. It is the one thing needed to bring order out of confusion in the psychic problems that interest so many at the present time.

This Great Secret, this *Master's Word,* was known to and preserved in the Mysteries of Antiquity, and is embodied and preserved in the traditions and symbols of Masonry today. This fact has been stated repeatedly in the body of this little book, the real purpose of which was to set students, and particularly masonic students, to searching for the real secret. It is the reward of study and devotion, and has never been obtained on any other terms. It has never been conferred in the ritualistic degrees of the Lodge, and never will or can be. It is the establishment of *understanding* in the soul of man between that higher self in him, and the More, and the Beyond self from which he draws his life, and from which his intuitions spring. This is real Initiation: Becoming: At-one-ment.

The author is both gratified and encouraged at the reception accorded and the interest manifested in this little book, and the commendations received from many quarters. That it could become, in any broad sense, popular, he never for a moment imagined. It is too serious and void of sensationalism for that. In entering now on its third thousand, it has already exceeded any expectation of the author, who will be profoundly gratified if he may aid, though it be but a little, in increasing the respect entertained by the community at large for the Order of Freemasonry, and encourage his brother Masons in seeking More Light.

I believe that nowhere amongst men today can there be found so near an approach to an Ideal Brotherhood of Man as in the Masonic Lodges. Perfect it is not, and cannot be till human evolution is completed. Among the hundreds of thousands of Masons today in the United States it would be difficult to find one who does not strive his best to exercise charity and loving-kindness, particularly toward his brothers in the Lodge. There are thousands of Masons, moreover, who realize that Masonry contains and implies far more than appears in the ritual and ceremonies of the Lodge. There is a very widespread and growing interest in this direction, and it is this that Mystic Masonry, above all else, is designed to foster, encourage, and help. Indeed, the growth of this feeling in the past decade is remarkable, and the present writer has not a shadow of a doubt as to the result.

It is the ethical precepts inculcated in the Lodge and so largely practiced by the craft, more than all else, that open the higher intuitions of man, and so enable him to grasp and finally comprehend the higher problems concealed in the profound symbolism of Masonry. Modern Masonry is thus fast becoming, like its ancient prototype, a School of the Mysteries; the real Mystery being the origin and nature of the human soul, and the transcendent and immortal destiny of Man.

The Masonic organization is so large, so widespread, so strong; its spirit so fraternal; its teaching so helpful and inspiring, that it seems destined to achieve the most glorious results in the encouragement and uplifting of the whole human race.

The hard and fast lines that have heretofore segregated mankind are rapidly disappearing. Creed and dogma have lost their hold since the State no longer protects them, and the anathemas of ecclesiastics are no longer feared. Men and women of all classes are coming into closer touch with the avowed purpose of understanding, in order that they may help each other. It is more and more recognized that the good of one is the welfare of all. The "sin of separateness" is thus slowly being undermined. Hence the ethical, the religious, the economic, and the political problems are seen to be practically inseparable, and all definitely related in the one problem of the higher evolution of man. This recognized unity of knowledge and community of interests is the prelude to the Universal

Brotherhood of man that is the ideal state and the dream of every true philanthropist throughout the ages. Masonry stands for just this, and all this, just as for ages the Great Mysteries clearly defined and promulgated the philosophy which makes such an ideal state, such a Great Republic of Nations and peoples possible. It must be founded on a knowledge of man's entire nature, and cemented by loving-kindness toward each and all, then only can it exist and endure.

To promote this glorious result is the sole purpose of this little book. This is indeed the *Work* of the Lodge, as it should be of every Frater throughout the world, till in the end it is the work of every individual.

Cincinnati, *January*, 1903.

Preface to the Second Edition

That a second edition of this little book should be called for within six weeks of the date of issue is, perhaps, the best answer to the inquiry in the mind of its author as to what kind of a reception so serious a view of modern Freemasonry, and so high an estimate of Ancient Mysteries as is herein set forth, might receive. It has not only attracted attention and excited inquiry, but met the unqualified approval of certain high Masons. Sir Albert Pike's greatest work, restricted to the members of the craft, obtained but one hundred and fifty subscribers. If Mystic Masonry quadrupled this subscription list before the date of publication, the reason is to be sought, not in the superior quality of the book, but in the more popular form in which the subject is handled, in the removal of all restrictions as to subscribers, and still more, from the fact that a widespread interest has of late arisen in regard to these subjects; offering, as the author believes, the grandest opportunity presented to real Masonry for more than a thousand years, for presenting its sublime philosophy to the world for the uplifting of humanity.

Mystic Masonry is, to a considerable extent, a compilation. It was not the author's purpose to become an innovator, but rather, in a modest way, an inspirer and renovator, and for this purpose he but repeated statements that had already been made by those high in Masonic authority, statements that had been overlooked or forgotten, and that needed to be remembered. In his preface to *Morals and Dogma,* Mr. Pike declares that about one-half of that work is original matter, and half taken from various sources, and that as he was writing neither for fame nor money, but for the benefit of the craft, the source of what he had set down was a matter of secondary importance. He often adapted, rather than quoted, in many places, and very seldom gave authorities. He wrote those things which he evidently believed his Masonic Brotherhood ought to know, and as he had divested his mind of all selfish motive or hope of gain, so must he be exempt from the charge of plagiarism. He drew very largely, in many places, from the writings of Abbé Constant, better known as Eliphas Levi, whose writings then existed only in the French language, and which undoubtedly contain the most profound knowledge of the Occult Sciences and the Ancient Mysteries given to the world since the days of the Old Initiates. As the present author has observed, in the body of this book, it matters far less whence these truths have been derived than what they really mean, although no reader is bound to accept the interpretation put upon them by any writer or commentator. Yet every intelligent inquirer may discern their general reasonableness, the logical sequence of the whole as revealing a profound philosophy of Nature and of Life, and the beneficent influence they must exert if universally diffused and generally adopted amongst men.

Liberty and Equality based on Fraternity may have degenerated into a slogan of blood in the days of the French Revolution, yet in more peaceful times must such Fraternity be interpreted as the ideal state, and made to promote the Universal and Unqualified Brotherhood of Man.

Introduction

The object of the author of this book is to show the relation between Freemasonry and the Mysteries of Antiquity. This much, at least, is implied by the title of the book. That there is both a historical and philosophical thread uniting these departments of human thought and action is well known to every intelligent student of Masonry, no less than to all students of Symbolism and Mysticism. One traveler, in the wilds of South America, records the fact that he found there an ancient roadbed running over mountain and valley for hundreds of miles. By whom this ancient structure was built is a matter of conjecture. It is now broken by time, with great gaps here and there, and forest trees obliterating its pathway, but it everywhere shows the designing hand of man. In like manner when we undertake to follow the landmarks than connect the ancient wisdom with modern times, we must not look for uninterrupted threads, yet nevertheless will the careful student find the lines of transmission unmistakable, and the interruptions no bar to the proof of transmission from age to age.

Masonry deals largely with the ethics and symbolism of the Ancient Mysteries. The writer believes that through the well-timed efforts of Masons today the grandest achievements in knowledge ever gained by man, which were originally concealed in the Greater Mysteries of Antiquity, and in time became lost to the world, may be again recovered. In the strictest sense this knowledge has never really been lost, as there have always existed those who were possessed of the Great Secret. It was originally veiled in order to conceal it from the profane, and written in a universal language of Symbolism that the wise among all nations and throughout all time might read it, as it were, in their own language. It was also written in parable and allegory, so that the unlettered and common people might not be deprived of its wise precepts, and of its force in shaping character, dissipating ignorance, and inspiring hope. This Ancient Wisdom is the fountain from which Masonry takes its rise. The true Science of Symbolism in time became lost; the Temples of Initiation fell into decay, or were destroyed by priests and potentates, jealous of their influence. For many weary centuries men have been trying to recover the lost key and to restore the ancient wisdom from the parables and allegories in which it had been concealed. But progress in this inverse order is not only necessarily slow and uncertain, but all such attempts have, more or less, given rise to fantastic flights of the imagination, and resulted in confusion, rather than in enlightenment. The result has been to bring the whole subject under contempt, and to make the name "mysticism" mean something vague and uncertain, if not altogether foolish, to those ignorant of its true meaning.

"Remember," says Bro. Albert Pike, "that the lessons and ceremonies of these degrees (those of the Blue-Lodge) have been for ages more and more accommodating themselves, by curtailment and sinking into common-place, to the often limited memory and capacity of the Master and Instructor, and to the intellect and needs of the Pupil and Initiate; that they have come to us from an age when symbols were used, not to reveal but to conceal: when the commonest learning was confined to a select few, and the simplest principles of morality seemed newly discovered truths: and that these antique and simple degrees now stand like the broken columns of a roofless, Druidic temple in their mutilated greatness: in many parts also corrupted by time, and disfigured by modern additions and absurd interpretations." — *Morals and Dogma,* p. 106.

Here, then, are two causes that have operated to render the old wisdom difficult of recovery, viz., concealment, and ignorant alteration or misinterpretation. To these must be added a third source of obliteration, viz., the direct efforts of interested parties to utterly destroy all records. "Let one only think of the thousands, and perhaps millions, of MSS. burnt; of monuments with their too indiscreet inscriptions and pictorial symbols pulverized to dust; of the bands of early hermits and ascetics roaming about among the ruined cities of Upper and Lower Egypt, in desert and mountain, valley and highlands, seeking for and ready to destroy every obelisk and pillar, scroll or parchment they could lay their hands upon, if it only bore the symbol of the tau or any other sign borrowed and appropriated by the new faith: — and he will then see plainly how it is that so little has remained of the records of the Past." — *Secret Doctrine, p. xl., vol.* I.

Every intelligent and unbiased Mason is more or less aware of these facts, and of the great difficulty attending all efforts to recover the Lost Word, and to rebuild the City and Temple of the Lord, — a glyph that has many meanings. The author of this book desires to aid all that he can in this noble and glorious undertaking.

In the effort to bring about such a result it is not contemplated that any innovations whatever should be introduced into Masonry as now organized. If the sublime philosophy which is the heritage of Masonry shall become universally diffused and rendered capable of apprehension by all intelligent persons, not only among Masons, but everywhere, its beneficent influence may thus become universal among men. In this way may be hastened the rise of that Great "Republic of which every Nation is a family, and every individual a child."

It will be very naturally questioned whether any thing can be definitely ascertained regarding the Greater Mysteries of Antiquity, inasmuch as they were always concealed, never revealed to the profane, never published to the world, and only recorded in glyph, parable and allegory. It has already been shown that all attempts to discover the real secret by running backward from parable and allegory have resulted in confusion and discouragement.

The interpretations resulting have been as fantastic and varied as the genius of each investigator; had any of these been possessed of a universal key to symbolism, or a complete philosophy of the Secret Doctrine, the result might have been very different. The solution of this question is not only greatly simplified, when investigation is guided by such a philosophy, or a complete key, but the investigator has the positive assurance at every step that he is on firm ground.

But a far more important consideration remains to be noted. There is a tradition in the far East, and to be often traced more or less vaguely in the West, that the Great Lodge of the Magi, the Adepts, the Perfect Masters, known and designated also by many other names, has never ceased to exist; that this Lodge has often, though secret and unknown, shaped the course of Empire and controlled the fate .of Nations. Knowing always the line of least resistance, and when and how to act, and having always in view only one object, viz., the Progress of Humanity and the Brotherhood of Man; despising fame and worldly honors, and working "without the hope of fee or reward," they have concealed their labors, and either influenced those who knew them not to do their work, or worked through agents pledged to conceal their very existence.

To the public generally, this may be a matter of little interest or importance, as the character of the work done must be the sole criterion by which that work is to be measured. But to Masons it should be of interest, as showing what it is to be indeed a Master Builder. It will reveal to them the meaning and goal of human evolution, and give them the unqualified assurance that that evolution is being now aided *by those who know,* as it has not been for many centuries. Such work has now become possible, because of a cycle of liberality and enlightenment, when the workers are not likely to be sacrificed to the Moloch of bigotry and superstition. Granting that such Masters exist, and that they are possessed of profound knowledge, that they are ready to help the world, the world must be ready and willing to receive such help, if it is to be benefited by it, instead of destroying its agents. Guided, then, by a complete philosophy; armed with a key to symbolism, and aided by these Grand Masters, the Lost Mysteries of Antiquity may be restored and made to tell their hoary secrets for the benefit of the coming age.

The object of this book is to give an outline of such work; it is introductory, and, to some extent, explanatory, but by no means exhaustive. It is not based upon any authority beyond the author's sincere convictions and capacity to apprehend the subject. The Mason who is ready to dig deeper and fill in the outline here furnished is recommended to read carefully, if he has not already done so, Albert Pike's great book, *Morals and Dogma.*

The historical method of research is not followed in the compilation or writing of this book, although historical facts are herein recorded. It is of far less importance to determine whence Masonry has been derived, than *what it really teaches.* In answering this question, it may be justly charged that the author has put his own interpretation forward, not against facts or history, but in the face of what may be regarded as insufficient historical proof. To such a charge he would reply, first, that no well-authenticated history of Masonry is known to exist; there being only isolated facts, or fragments, recording the existence of certain organizations or movements at different times, and their disappearance on account of inward dissension or outward persecution. Then another movement would spring up, at another time and place, and perhaps under a different name, though evidently working on the same general lines, only to meet with a similar fate. One writer makes the statement that fully eight hundred different degrees have thus, from time to time, been introduced to the Craft as Masonic. In no case does there exist any reliable consecutive history of these various movements. But even if such history existed, it would but little serve the purpose of the present work, as will be readily seen from what has heretofore been said regarding all these attempts to discover the Lost Word, by reading backward from the outer form of Symbolism. Such a history would be curious and interesting, as showing the fertility of the human imagination, and its proneness to regard as valuable that which is curious and fantastic, because it is concealed. Mere vulgar curiosity and secrecy alone have never yet been the pass-words to the *Adytum* of real Initiation. On the other hand, such a history, did it really exist, would be tinged with a touch of pathos, on account of the many sorrowful disappointments it would have to record, in the case of earnest souls seeking, with sincerity and in truth, for the "Lost Word of the Master," only to be overwhelmed at last by disappointment, or to be publicly executed as malefactors and enemies of State or Church. Such histories as exist well deserve, in many cases, the designation of "organized fiction," and almost invariably record merely the opinions of those who were friendly or unfriendly to such movements, with a corresponding dearth of facts.

For these reasons, no specially historical character is attempted to be given to this work. One of the strong points urged by the writer is the logical inferences drawn from such facts as are known to exist, and the general spirit everywhere admitted as pervading the Ancient Mysteries in their original purity. That such organizations should exist through all time and yet be without a history seems at first a strange paradox. The enemies of Masonry will urge this fact as a reason for rejecting all that is herein contained, ignorant of the fact that few histories of any people or any epoch are better founded. Foremost among these detractors or deniers will be found the bigoted sectarian and the modern materialist. With each of these the real genius of Masonry is in perpetual conflict. For the first, the universal and unqualified Brotherhood of Man, is a dead letter, for he believes that only himself and his chosen associates can be saved. For the second, the materialist, the recognition of the Divine Architect of the Universe, in Masonry, as the *"Principle of Principles,"* and belief in the immortality of the Soul, will prove an equal stumbling block. Fortunately, the number of bigoted sectarians and the out-and-out materialists is few. The historical deficiency referred to is by no means without a parallel. That superstructure known as Christianity has, it is true, many historical phases; of dogmas the most contradictory; of doctrines promulgated in one age, and enforced with vice-regal authority, and severe penalties for denial and disbelief, only to be denied and repudiated as "damnable heresy" in another age. In the meantime, the origin of these doctrines and the personality of the *Man of Sorrows* around which these traditions cluster receive no adequate support from authentic history. What, then, shall we conclude regarding the real genius of Christianity? Is it all a fable, put forth and kept alive by designing men, to support their pretensions to authority? Are historical facts and personal biography alone entitled to credit? While everlasting principles, Divine Beneficence, and the laying down of one's life for another are of no account? Is that which has inspired the hope and brightened the lives of the down-trodden and despairing for ages a mere fancy, a designing lie? Tear every shred of history from the life of the *Christ* today, and prove beyond all controversy that he never existed, and Humanity, from its heart-of-hearts, would create him again tomorrow and justify the creation by every intuition of the human soul and by every need of the daily life of man. The historical contention might be given up, ignored, and the whole character, genius, and mission of *Jesus,* the *Christ,* be none the less real, beneficent, and eternal, with all of its human and dramatic episodes. Explain it as you will, it can never be explained away; the character remains; and whether Historical or Ideal, it is *real* and *eternal.*

This digression serves to illustrate a principle of interpretation. The Traditions and Symbols of Masonry do not derive their real value from historical data, but *from the universal and eternal truths which they embody*. Were they historical episodes only, the world in its cyclic revolutions would long ago have swept by them and buried them in eternal oblivion. These great truths, obscured and lost in one age by misinterpretation or persecution, rise, Phoenix-like, rejuvenated in the next. They are *Immortal Ideals,* knowing neither decay nor death. They are like a Divine Image concealed in a block of stone (the rough ashler), which many artists assail with mallet and chisel, square and compass, only, perchance, to release a distorted idol. Only the Perfect Master can so chip away the stone as to reveal in all its grandeur and beauty the *Divine Ideal,* and endow it with the breath of life. Such is the building of character. The fable of Pygmalion and Galatea is, after all, more real than history. The thread of history is not in isolated facts, joined by conjecture, and warped to the ignorant, bigoted, and time-serving opinions of men. The real thread is to be sought in the *theme* that runs through the symphony of creation; in the lofty *Ideals* that inspire the life of man, and that lead him from the clod and the lowlands, where hover the ghosts of superstition and fear, to the mountains of light, where dwell forever inspiration and peace. Such ideals are the *Christ, Hiram,* and the *Perfect Master.*

It is doubtful whether any portion of the present organization of Masonry, as such, can be traced further back than the middle of the 17th century. The great Masonic revolution of 1717, and the Constitutions of 1723 and 1738, seem to have brought into existence the present organizations; which, by no means uniform throughout the world, have, nevertheless, very much in common. There were indeed earlier organizations, often unknown and unsuspected, and operating under different names, while using the same glyphs and symbolism; but no direct connection has been clearly shown to exist between these organizations and those of the present time. But as our pursuit is philosophical rather than historical, and our appeal rather to reason than to authority, we need not go into these matters further than may be necessary as landmarks in following our philosophical thread.

A distinctively Christian character is now given to some of the Masonic degrees in Europe and America. Without the slightest opposition to the Christian religion, as such, it can readily be shown that a sectarian bias of any kind is an innovation, wholly unwarranted, and entirely contrary to the genius of Masonry. Masonry, on the broad principle of toleration and brotherhood, can exclude neither Jew nor Gentile, Parsee nor Buddhist from its ample fold. Masonry is chiefly indebted to the French Jesuits for the distinctively Christian character of some of its degrees. The templar degrees are purely sectarian, and can in no sense claim that universal character which recognizes the fraternity of all religions, and finds fellowship with all men, as brothers of one common humanity. No genuine Mason, imbued with the spirit of liberality, will treat any religion with derision or contempt, or exclude from membership any Brother who believes in the existence of God, the Brotherhood of Man, and the Immortality of the Soul. This Catholic spirit is the very foundation of Masonry, and any departure from it is un-Masonic, and subversive of the ancient Landmarks and Genius of Masonry. If the Catholic Priests have the right to Christianize Masonry, so have Jews, Buddhists, or Mohammedans, an equal right to transform it to fit their own creeds; and such transformation in every case deprives Masonry of its universal character. While it cannot benefit the creed to which Masonry is made to conform, it will, in the end, destroy Masonry itself. True Masonry has, for ages, held aloft the torchlight of Toleration, Equity and Fraternity. The bigoted sectarian, whoever he may be, divides the world into two classes: those who, with zeal and blind faith, accept his dogmas, and those who do not. The first he calls "brothers," the second class he regards as aliens, if not enemies. Masonry, while adopting no religion and no form of doctrine or creed, as such, or as formulated by any one religion, recognizes certain basic principles embodying the ethics taught in all religions. Every Mason may formulate his creed to suit himself, and may institute such forms of worship as may seem to him desirable or beneficent. Now, that the old creeds are everywhere losing their hold and falling in pieces, it is more than ever necessary to show that none of these have ever been a legitimate part of Masonry; that while Masonry antagonizes none, it can adopt none as Masonic. This impartial spirit is the basis of that impartial justice illustrated in more than one Masonic degree.

"The distinction between the esoteric and exoteric doctrines (a distinction purely Masonic) was always and from the very earliest times preserved among the Greeks. It remounted to the fabulous time of Orpheus...And after the time of Alexander they resorted for instruction, dogmas, and mysteries, to all the schools; to those of Egypt and Asia, as well as those of ancient Thrace, Sicily, Etruria, and Attica."

The real source from whence the Ancient Wisdom came was Persia and old India, the Mother of Civilizations and Religions, and of the esoteric or concealed wisdom.

In this book it is not attempted to explain all of the symbols of Freemasonry, or to completely unfold the philosophy of the Secret Doctrine. Such an undertaking would transcend both the time and ability of the author. The aim is rather to show a few points of contact, to outline methods of interpretation, to convince the unbiased reader that in the ancient mysteries lies a mine of wisdom far beyond all modern achievement, and to invite the cooperation of Masons in upholding these Ancient Truths. To recover the *Lost Word* is to revive the Ancient Wisdom, and this will facilitate Universal Fraternity and Universal Progress more than all other agencies now in our possession.

In its ritualism and monitorial lessons Masonry teaches nothing in morals, in science, in religion, or in any other department of human knowledge or human interest, not taught elsewhere in current forms of thought, or by the sages of the past. In these directions it has no secrets of any kind. It is in the ancient symbols of Freemasonry that its real secrets lie concealed, and these are as densely veiled to the Mason as to any other, unless he has studied the science of symbolism in general, and masonic symbols in particular. In place of the term Mystic Masonry, the term Symbolic Masonry might have been used alone, but just here lies the whole secret, a profound mystery, and few Masons up to the present time have had the interest or the patience necessary to such investigation. This is a fact, and not intended as either a criticism or a reproach. If lacking a knowledge of the profound meaning of masonic symbolism, and its transcendent interest and importance, Masons have allowed the whole organization not only to fail in all real progress, but to degenerate, that is indeed a reproach. The number of individuals admitted to fellowship in the various degrees can not atone for such degeneracy, but on the contrary it rather emphasizes it. The author of this book is perfectly well aware that such a treatise will not be popular with a certain class of Masons. They are almost certain to regard it with contempt and to undertake to frown it down. They will make the statement, which is perfectly true, that no such meaning has before been explained to them, and that no such philosophy is found in the monitorial instructions of the Lodge. The author can not, therefore, be justly accused of revealing any of the secrets of the Lodge unlawfully. The most profound secrets of Masonry are not revealed in the Lodge at all. They belong only to the few. This again, if admitted as a fact, will seem an injustice. But these secrets must be sought by the individual himself, and the candidate is debarred from possessing them solely by his own inattention to the hints everywhere given in the ritual of the Lodge, or by his indifference to the subject. If he prefers to treat the whole subject with contempt, and to deny that any such real knowledge exists, it becomes evident that he not only closes the door against the possibility of himself possessing such knowledge, but he also becomes impervious to any evidence of its existence that might come to him at any time. He has no one but himself to blame if he is left in darkness.

On the other hand, there is a large and increasing number of persons among Masons who really desire more light; who are satisfied that there must be other and profounder meanings behind the ritual and ceremonies of the Lodge. Some of these have taken the hint and "Journeyed Eastward" in search of Light.

The play made upon the word *"light,"* in the Royal Arch, and in almost every other degree; the three greater lights, and the three lesser, ought to teach every intelligent Mason that *Light,* and the trinity, or triangle of lights, have a profound meaning, or else that the whole ritual is a meaningless farce. Aside from all interest that any individual Mason may find in the subject for his own enlightenment, it is obviously his duty, while preserving unaltered the usages and landmarks of the Order, to advance the interests and fame of Masonry itself by every just and benevolent means in his power. The names that are honored in the traditions of the Lodge and in the history of the Order, belong to those who have thus achieved enduring fame, and they are held aloft in the ritual of the Lodge as worthy of all emulation. But shall neither the present nor the future add anything to this roll of honor? or, if need be, to the list of martyrs? Are the days of noble deeds past with Masonry forever? and the need of self-sacrifice and devotion altogether a thing of the past? There was never greater need than at the present time; never so great an opportunity as now for Masonry to assume its true place among the institutions of man and to force recognition by the simple power of Brotherly Love, Relief, and Truth, based upon philosophy such as nowhere else exists outside of its ancient symbols. If the majority of Masons do not realize the true significance and value of their possessions, there is all the more need for those who do to speak out, even in the face of discouragement and detraction, and do their utmost to demonstrate the truth. Does any intelligent Mason imagine that the guilds of practical Masons of a century and a half ago originated the Order of Freemasons? There were indeed Architects and Master Builders among them, but the great majority of Masons were far more ignorant, as manual servants, than the majority of such builders are today. Freemasonry is modeled on the plan of the Ancient Mysteries, with their glyphs and allegories, and this is no mere coincidence; the parallels are too closely drawn. Bro.

Pike came to the conclusion, after long and patient investigation, that certain Hermetic Philosophers had a hand in the construction of the organization of Free and Accepted Masons, and if they embodied in its symbolism more than appears on the surface, and far deeper truths than the superficial student readily discerns, it was evidently designed that future generations should discern and use these profounder secrets. The evidence in this direction is not only conclusive but overwhelming, though only fragments of it can be here adduced.

In brief, then, the real secrets of Freemasonry lie in its Symbols, and the meaning of the symbols reveals a profound philosophy, and a universal science, that have never been transcended by man.

The author of this book is not presumptive enough to claim that he has exhausted, or altogether apprehended, in its entirety, this old philosophy. He has, however, found such interest in its study, and it has opened to him such a mine of wealth, with such treasures revealed at every step, that he desires to share these precious jewels with his fellow craftsmen, that they may also go further, and from the secret vaults bring forth for inspection other and greater discoveries. These jewels have not been concealed by accident, but by design, in order that they might, in some future age, be restored. Even the *stone* that was rejected, and became lost in the rubbish, not only bears an emblem, and contains a mark, but is itself, from first to last, with its surroundings, method of restoration, and final use, a symbol. It is the center of a five-pointed star, which is the kabalistic sign of man. In one direction, it symbolizes the five senses, lost in the rubbish of passion and selfish gratification. When this rejected or lost stone is recovered, and sent to the King of the temple (man's Higher-Self), and is recognized and restored, the arch is complete, and the gateway of the senses gives entrance to the "Palace of the King." The result is light or illumination. Such are the *Illuminati*.

The writing of this book has been altogether a labor of love. It is designed to be no less a tribute to the Heroes and Martyrs of Masonry in the Past, than an humble offering to the Fraternity of the Present.

J. D. B.
Cincinnati, *November* 9, 1896.

Chapter One - Principles of Education and Ethics

"And this to fill us with regard far man
With apprehension of his passing worth,
Desire to work his proper nature out,
And ascertain his rank and final place.
For these things tend still upward, progress is
The Law of life; man is not Man as yet.
Nor shall I deem his object served, his end
Attained, his genuine strength put fairly forth,
While only here and there a star dispels
The darkness; here and there a towering mind
O'erlooks its prostrate fellows; when the host
Is out at once to the despair of night;
When all mankind alike is perfected,
Equal in full-blown powers, then, not till then,
I say, begins men's general infancy."

— Browning's *Paracelsus*.

So long as the struggle for bare existence involves, as it does today, the greater part of the energy, time, and opportunities of man, he will never discover the real meaning of manhood, or the purpose of human existence. Even this much may be discerned from physical evolution alone; from the study of the human brain, in which there is a continually increasing portion of gray substance set free from the functions incident to the preservation of the physical structure, and evidently designed to be appropriated to separate and higher uses. Mere intellectual activities alone, connected with the physical plane, with the maintenance and enjoyment of life, will not explain the philosophy of cerebral development. It is largely for this reason that the offices of the encephalon are so little known today. There are latent powers and almost infinite capabilities in man, the meaning of which he has hardly yet dreamed of possessing. Nor will leisure and intellectual cultivation alone reveal these powers. It is only through a complete philosophy of the entire nature of man and the capacities and destiny of the human soul, supplemented by the use of such knowledge, that man will eventually come into the possession of his birthright; and from this "general infancy" — as Browning puts it — begin the journey from real manhood to perfection.

Two conditions at the present time stand squarely in the way of such achievements: first, anarchy and confusion, the result of selfishness in all social relations. This condition can be overcome in but one way, viz., by the recognition of the unqualified Brotherhood of Man; not as a theory, a religious duty, or a mere matter of sentiment; but as a fact in Nature; a universal and Divine Law; the penalty for the violation of which is precisely the conditions under which humanity now suffers.

The second condition, which has given rise to "Confusion among the Workmen" in building the social temple and the individual habitation of man, is false ideals; inefficient methods of education; and almost total ignorance of the existence and the nature of the soul. The result of this ignorance may be seen in the fact, that not one individual in a million who has both leisure and opportunity, makes any real advancement in the evolution of the higher powers; or is even cognizant of the fact that he is a living soul. Old age is filled, not only with infirmities, but with miseries without number. Not one in a million can say with the poet:

"Tis the sunset of life, gives me mystical lore;
  As coming events cast their shadows before."

In the great majority of cases with the aged, death is looked upon with uncertainty or fear, or as a blessed release from suffering and sorrow. Life is thus endured as a necessary evil, and is more often voted by the individual to be a failure than a success. What life ought to be is often conceived from our many failures; what it might be is dimly perceived from the intuitions of the soul which the struggles and selfishness of existence have failed to entirely obliterate.

These things ought not so to be, nor need they longer be, if earnest men and women would seek diligently, first for the cause of all our ills, and secondly, for a sufficient remedy. This remedy is to be found, first, in Knowledge; second, in Service of the Truth. Let us now examine a little more in detail some of the conditions under which we suffer.

The present is proudly designated as the Age of Science. The art of printing, the power of Steam and Electricity in applied science; the Conservation and Correlation of Energy, and the Theory of Evolution in speculative science, with the resulting details, constitute the greater part of our real discoveries. One machine is made to do the work of a score or more of men, while the laborers who have been thus displaced have no adequate share in the profits of mechanical invention. Those who work with their hands are no longer artisans, but generally machines, a necessity as to different details for which no machine has yet been invented. The work of the laboring classes is thus reduced to the routine of drudgery without the hope of advancement; and, therefore, with no other incentive than to keep the wolf from the door. A manufactured article which, when completed, serves more often to foster extravagance and luxury than to supply a necessity, passes through many hands before it is completed. The laborer is glad even thus to serve, because idleness means starvation, and still the Army of the Unemployed is an ever-increasing host. The occupation of the common laborer is even more precarious than that of the mechanic or the artisan. Is it any wonder, then, that in times of financial uncertainty, when thousands of laborers are out of employment and threatened with starvation, unable to apprehend the real causes of their suffering, naturally envious of those who are supplied with all the luxuries of life, and knowing that *something* is radically wrong somewhere to produce all of this inequality and injustice, band together to secure what they conceive to be their rights by force?

But all this concerns mere physical existence, though the effects are seen on every plane of life. With regard to the Science of Man, and all that concerns his origin, nature and destiny, individually or collectively, neither science nor religion has taught us anything. Science has given us the slogan — "the survival of the fittest," — a mere scientific phrasing of the motto of the Robber Barons, that "he may seize who hath the power, and he may hold who can." In the industries of life the result may be reduced to one word, Competition. In manufacture, in trade, in all professions — even the Clerical profession — in schools, everywhere, Competition, Strife, and "the survival of the fittest."

> "And this to fill us with regard for man;
>   With apprehension of his passing worth,
>   Desire to work his proper nature out,
>   And ascertain his rank and final place."

So far our boasted civilization is, on a gigantic scale, a Car of *Jagannatha,* and it crushes heads and hearts as relentlessly as the wooden idol of our heathen brothers, only, American-like, we do the killing by wholesale.

Are not nearly the whole of the energies and activities of life directed to and expended upon the physical plane alone? And has not the struggle for existence increased with the great majority, in spite of all our boasted progress, our boasted science, and our Christian Civilization? We have neither the time, the energy, nor the disposition to discover the real meaning and aim of life, because all our energies are absorbed in the bare maintenance of existence.

> "Ah! small is the pleasure existence can give,
>   When the fear we shall die only proves that we live."

If real knowledge of the nature of the soul and the destiny of man had never existed, our present condition would be pitiable in the extreme; but when it is demonstrated that this knowledge once existed, that it was first degraded by selfishness and then lost by design, and that for centuries designing Priests, many of whom would have disgraced a scaffold, but who have been canonized as saints, have done their utmost to deprive humanity of this knowledge, what shall the humanitarian say? Shall he preach Universal Brotherhood and Toleration, and yet seek revenge on the priesthood? A thousand times, no! but rather leave priest and proletariat to settle their own affairs and go their own way, and go to work *ourselves* to recover the *lost knowledge,* and when recovered devote it absolutely to Humanity.

The most hopeful sign of the times is the humanitarian work being done by thousands of well-disposed persons who appreciate existing evils, and desire to get rid of them. In very few instances, however, the results attained are commensurate with the energy or the sacrifice employed, for self-sacrifice is a virtue not altogether unknown to Christendom. But in very many instances these humanitarian efforts resemble an attempt to destroy a Upas tree, which being cut down every day grows again before morning. We imprison and execute criminals, and crime nowhere decreases. We sequestrate and "doctor" the insane, and insanity continually increases. We build hospitals for orphans, the sick and the aged, and we do well; but orphanage, sickness and the distress and poverty of age grow in no wise less. It ought sometime to occur to us that society is all wrong, or that something is radically wrong with all our methods. In the aggregate all the profits derived from scientific discoveries and from labor-saving machines has to be returned to the criminal or indigent classes. The only thing that we can boast of as a result is an increase in the number of millionaires; and these, as a class, instead of being the fruition of a higher evolution are almost without exception the very flower of a Civilization of Competition and Selfishness. They have created an aristocracy of wealth, very often by gambling or stealing, and determine the criterion of what is called "good society," viz.: extravagant display and vulgar pretentiousness.

What then is really the matter with our boasted civilization? The answer is, ignorance and selfishness; it is the result of the "Sin of Separateness."

If in our social and political affairs the foregoing are the results in spite of all scientific progress, and in the face of our boasted "Christian Civilization," in the intellectual realm, or in educational matters, are we any better off? Let us see.

One of the first lessons the child is taught in school is Competition. It is instilled into every child at an early age that he should aim to be at the head of his class, and his exertions are continually incited to get ahead of his fellows. Many a young man or young woman graduating from literary institutions and carrying off the prizes for proficiency or scholarship are mental wrecks all the rest of their lives. Nor are the subjects taught, or the branches of learning mastered, such, in a great majority of instances, as are of any great practical value to the student in after life. The amount of technical information acquired is often useful in the so-called learned professions; but in the ordinary walks of life more often fall into disuse, and seldom serve the purpose of opening the higher avenues of knowledge, or putting the individual in possession of a real knowledge of himself.

Herbert Spencer mentions five objects to be attained in the education of children: That education which prepares for direct self-preservation; that which prepares for indirect self-preservation; that which prepares for parenthood; that which prepares for citizenship; and that which prepares for the miscellaneous refinements of life. These objects set forth by one of the most profound writers of the present time, may be seen to pertain to self-preservation and "getting on" in life, the last object may, by implication, have a Social bearing; but any higher knowledge, designed to put man in possession of his real powers and to promote the evolution of the soul, are not even mentioned.

In all our religious instruction, from childhood, and through all the ministrations of religion in after life, we are taught to look very sharp after the salvation of our own souls; and this in the face of the statement that a very large proportion of the human race will eventually be utterly lost, or damned, for all eternity! Science completes the picture by trying to demonstrate that the struggle for existence is a necessary condition of all improvement; and that only the sharpest tooth and the longest claw can survive. The ideal thus held aloft by both religion and science is selfishness. Self-preservation is regarded as the "first law of life." The result is materialism in the strictest and broadest sense, and this has paralyzed, where it has not utterly destroyed, all higher ideals.

Is it not reasonable to suppose that if we were possessed of real knowledge we might so govern our actions, and so shape our lives as to avoid the pitfalls of ignorance, and set our feet on the line of the higher evolution? Religion offers Faith, with a system of rewards and punishments, and inculcates Charity, which is more often interpreted as the giving of alms; but religion does not give us Knowledge. Science offers a theory, or a working hypothesis, but still does not give us Knowledge. So long as it requires all of our energies to barely maintain existence on the physical plane, and to help those who cannot do even that, unaided, we have little opportunity to seek for higher things.

The complicated system under which we are working is the result of many centuries of ignorance and superstition, and of many generations of evildoing, and these results cannot be changed in a day. Many of our modern institutions, covered over, as they are, with abuses and injustice, are, nevertheless, so deep-rooted that they will have to work themselves out to the bitter end of pain, sorrow, and, probably, through lawlessness and bloodshed. This *need* not be, yet it would be impossible to convince, all at once, a sufficient number of individuals who are involved in these institutions, of the real cause of all our misery, and, at the same time, to induce them to co-operate at once to remove the cause. Such a thing is not to be expected, because of universal unbelief as to the existence of the remedy proposed; hence, retributive Justice will have to work out its own results.

Is it really necessary that mankind should forever remain in ignorance, and forever repeat the same follies, and invite the retribution that we have invoked?

In the following pages, two sources of knowledge have been pointed out, viz., Masonry and Philosophy, and these have been shown to take their rise, either directly or indirectly, from the Mysteries of Antiquity. The Unqualified Brotherhood of Man is the basis of all Ethics, and the Great Republic is the Ideal State. If these concepts were accepted and acted upon, there would result time, opportunity, and the power to apprehend the deeper problems of the origin, nature, and destiny of man. "Man is not man as yet." What he may be, and what he might do, under favorable conditions, is very seldom even dreamed of. We never build beyond our ideals. We habitually fall below them.

There are a few persons in nearly every community with whom the struggle for existence is reduced to the minimum; and, undoubtedly, the majority of these are women. Having a competency against want, or being amply provided for, they really have leisure for study and self-improvement; and many of these engage more or less in charitable work. But possessing no high ideal beyond the meritoriousness of charity and the self-approbation which it brings, and having no real knowledge as to the nature of the soul and the laws of its higher evolution, they fritter away their opportunity in luxury and self-indulgence, which they feel is justified by the tribute they have already paid to charity. The result is, that they are habitually consumed with *ennui;* and they are as unstable as water in the search for a new sensation or a new excitement.

If the majority of these are women who determine the standards and usages in what is called "society," the ideals of their male associates are far lower than theirs, and the men are saved from *ennui* by the diversity of Club Life or the necessities of business. The common laborer who finds continued employment is really less miserable oftentimes than these sons and daughters of fortune, who generally lose all zest in life, whose old age is filled with misery over their vanished youth, and whose lives are frequently cut short by paresis, where they do not degenerate into imbecility. It is one of the most hopeful signs of the time that among this favored class an increasing number are found devoting themselves, their time, energy, and money, to the betterment of the condition of the masses. Reincarnation being true, these servants of humanity are laying by a store of good Karma, which is literally "treasure in heaven," and which must inevitably secure for them still broader opportunities and greater power for good in another life; and best of all, they are unfolding the higher spiritual perceptions. Nothing so shrouds the Higher Self in man as selfishness, and this is the reason why so few persons are possessed of the direct perception that what is true, is True, and that what is false, is False.

There has been for a long time a very widespread and increasing conviction that Education would prove a panacea for all our evils; and that if we could begin with the young, and have the training of children, we could eventually reform society, even though these children might be the offspring of vicious parentage. That "we must educate or we must perish" contains, no doubt, a great truth; but it is offset by another saying: "Education cannot repair the defects of birth." What real education is, how and when it should begin, and what, under the most favorable circumstances, it may be expected to accomplish, we do not yet perceive. The saying that it takes at least three generations to make a Gentleman contains a truth, even if the criterion as to what constitutes a real gentleman may be uncertain or defective. And again, the saying, that the education of a child should begin at least nine months before it is born, shows that prenatal conditions and influences are at least recognized as existing. But in this last direction, viz., as to the environment of the Mother during gestation, the Ancient Greeks knew far more than we, and enacted laws to prevent physical deformity from being propagated or even seen. The result was physical symmetry such as the world has seldom seen.

Now when all these problems are studied in the light of re-incarnation the greater part of all obscurity disappears. Such study teaches us what the Ego is, and exactly what is determined by heredity, and what are the individual and inalienable possessions of the Ego itself. It teaches how, by a law as blind as that of gravitation, because it is always absolutely just, and as inflexible as Fate, the Karma of the child, associates it with the Karma of the parents, whether on the score of virtue or of vice. If both vice and virtue adhere to the Ego as me result of all former living, and are manifest in the *tendencies* of the individual, one way or the other, then the parentage, in any case, can only furnish the necessary conditions of expression; the opportunity to work out the innate tendencies.

Now the thing that education can and ought to change, is these innate tendencies. This is the only genuine reformation; and a great step toward this is gained by improvement in individual environment. If, however, it be considered that all environment is the result of Karma under natural law, it will be seen that the most unfortunate and hopeless environment might sometimes afford the very conditions of reformation. It can be imagined that a really intelligent and aspiring Ego, brought by Karma into these unfavorable conditions as the result of its own acts in a former life, would not only put forth all of its energies to rise, but would be forevermore repelled by such degrading influences as now surround him, and flee from them as from a pestilence.

Here we come face to face with the real problem of education. How shall we educate? With the children of the poor, and even with many of those of the middle classes, the ordinary curriculum of School and College often serves to inculcate ideas of luxury and contempt for labor, and results, in many instances, in idleness and dissipation. Many parents are ambitious that their children should be educated, in order that they may escape from hard work, and have an easier time in life than they have had themselves. In morality, or ethics, the children are taught certain precepts, or are required to recite certain religious formula, such as the Creed or the Catechism; they are

28

very seldom, however, taught unselfishness or self-conquest. The result is that the innate perceptions of the child, which are naturally far keener than most people are aware of, and which invariably, unless cultivated, become blunted with age and worldly experience, are utterly disregarded, or they are blunted by the very system of competition in education to which reference has already been made. It may thus be seen that it makes all the difference in the world how we educate, and that Ideals here are of more importance than almost anywhere else.

It is true that in some of the newer colleges, methods are being introduced which foster individuality, and which cultivate the natural perceptions to an extent hitherto almost unknown. This method must necessarily result in putting those students who are so fortunate as to come under its influence in possession of their own faculties, and in making them aware of their own capabilities. This method must necessarily favor a strong Individuality in the student. Now, if this can be supplemented by a further knowledge of the Latent Powers of the Soul and with the true ideals of the higher evolution, the result will be something not yet apprehended by the majority of educators.

In discussing the question as to what kind of knowledge is of the most use, Herbert Spencer places Scientific Knowledge in the first category; not alone for its practical results, but on account of the ideals to which it may give rise, and the broader apprehension to which it may lead. "Only the sincere man of science," he says, "and not the mere calculator of distances, or analyzer of compounds, or labeler of species; but him who through lower truths seeks higher, and eventually the highest — can truly know how utterly beyond, not only human knowledge, but human conception, is the Universal Power of which Nature, and Life, and Thought are manifestations."

In like manner Professor Huxley makes the consummation of Science to be the discernment of the rational order pervading the universe. It is, then, our methods that are most at fault and our ignorance that holds us down.

It is this higher knowledge toward which all useful and rational acquirement tends; and why should our efforts cease short of the very highest? All education that does not tend in this direction, with the final goal consistently and continually in view, is false, and is necessarily a failure. Now, this higher knowledge is a knowledge of the Soul: of its origin, nature, powers, and the laws that govern its evolution; and this is precisely the knowledge which modern science fails to afford, but which Ancient Science taught in the Mysteries of Antiquity. All preliminary study and training led up to this — "The real measure of a man." Just as all life is an evolution, so is all real knowledge an initiation; and it proceeds in a natural order, and advances by specific "degrees." The candidate must always be worthy and well qualified, duly and truly prepared. That is, he must perceive that such knowledge exists; must desire to possess it; and must be willing to make whatever personal sacrifice is necessary for its acquirement. He must have passed beyond the stage of blind belief or superstition, the bondage of fear, the age of fable, and the dominion of appetite and sense. This is the meaning of being "duly and truly prepared." He must have proved his fitness in these directions, no less than the absence in him of that subtler form of intellectual selfishness which comes from the possession of knowledge, and the desire for dominion through it over others less highly endowed, for selfish purposes of his own. His motive, therefore, alone, can determine that he is "worthy and well qualified."

It is true on every plane of life, that in the process by which knowledge is acquired — always by experience — man *becomes* the thing which he knows; that is, knowing is a progressive *becoming*. There results, therefore, a continual transformation of the motives, ideals, and perceptions of the individual, whenever in his daily experience in life he is placed on the lines of least resistance or the Natural Order of Evolution. This is the really scientific and philosophical meaning of all *Initiation*. By referring to the chapter in which the *Principles* and *Planes* of Life are considered, it will be seen that the principle just stated is the logical deduction from the idea of Microcosm and Macrocosm, or the philosophical concept that man is Involved from Divinity, and Evolves with Universal Nature; and that, therefore, his evolution runs *pari passu* with that of the earth he inhabits.

There is so much of the commonplace that passes with us for knowledge, and that is so utterly void of comprehension, that unless one is familiar with this line of thought he will not readily see the truth and bearing of the statement, that man always becomes that which he really knows. Here lies the reason why the mere inculcation of moral precepts so often fails entirely in transforming character; and why there is so much lip-service. In his travels through China and Thibet, Abbe Hue gives a graphic account of the traveling traders whom he encountered. He depicts their shrewdness in trade and their general air of friendliness, and declares that the slogan forever on their lips was that "All men are brothers," but this did not prevent them from taking every possible advantage of their customers; so easy is it for a moral precept to degenerate into mere slang. Conscience is the struggle of the understanding in assimilating experience; it is the effort of the individual to adjust precept with practice, or in other words, Conscience is that living, active process, resulting in the growth of the soul, and in the increase of man's power to apprehend truth.

In the Ancient Mysteries, Life presented itself to the candidate as a problem to be solved, and not as certain propositions to be memorized and as easily forgotten. The solution of this problem constituted all genuine initiation, and at every step or degree the problem expanded. As the vision of the candidate enlarged in relation to the problems and meaning of life, his powers of apprehension and assimilation also increased proportionately. This was also an evolution. It may reasonably be supposed that the lower degrees of such initiation concerned the ordinary affairs of life, viz., a knowledge of the laws and processes of external nature: the candidate's relation to these through his physical body, and his relations, on the physical plane, through his animal senses, and social instincts, to his fellow-men. These matters being learned, adjusted, Mastered, the candidate passed to the next degree. Here he learned theoretically, at first, the nature of the soul; the process of its evolution, and began to unfold those finer instincts that have been so often referred to in certain sections of this work. If he was found capable of apprehending these, and kept his "vow" in the preceding degree, he presently discovered the evolution within him of senses and faculties pertaining to the "soul-plane." His progress would be instantly arrested, and his teachers would refuse all further instruction, if he was found negligent of the ordinary duties of life; those to his family, his neighbors, or his country. All these must have been fully discharged before he could stand upon the threshold as a candidate for the Greater Mysteries; for in these he became an unselfish Servant of Humanity as a whole; and had no longer the right to bestow the gifts of knowledge or power that he possessed, upon his own kinsmen, or friends, in preference to strangers. In the higher degrees, he might be precluded from using these powers even to preserve his own life. Both the Master and his Powers belong to Humanity. If the reader will but reflect a moment, how the tantalizing Jews called upon Jesus to "save himself and come down from the cross," if he were the Christ, it may be seen that this doctrine of Supreme Selflessness ought, long ago, to have been better apprehended by the Christian world; for while it is a Divine Attribute, the Synonym of the Christ, it is latent in all humanity, and must be evolved as herein described.

That which makes such an evolution seem to modern readers impossible, is, that it cannot be conceived as being accomplished in a single life, nor can it be. It is the result of persistent effort guided by high ideals through many lives. Those who deny Pre-existence may logically deny all such evolution. There must, however, come a time when the consummation is reached in one life; and this is the logical meaning of the saying of Jesus — it is finished.

Chapter Two - The Genius of Freemasonry

"The whole world is but one Republic, of which each Nation is a family, and every individual a child. Masonry, not in anywise derogating from the differing duties which the diversity of States requires, tends to create a new people, which, composed of men of many nations and tongues, shall all be bound together by the bonds of Science, Morality and Virtue." — Pike's *Morals and Dogma, p.* 220.

"In fine, the real object of this association (Freemasonry) may be summed up in these words: To efface from among men the prejudices of caste, the conventional distinctions of color, origin, opinion, nationality; to annihilate fanaticism and superstition, extirpate national discord, and with it extinguish the firebrand of war; in a word — to arrive, by free and pacific progress, at one formula or model of eternal and universal right, according to which each individual human being shall be free to develop every faculty with which he may be endowed, and to concur heartily and with the fullness of his strength, in the bestowment of happiness upon all, and thus to make of the whole human race one family of brothers, united by affection, wisdom and labor." — Rebold's *History of Masonry, p.* 62.

The above quotations from two of the most prominent modern writers on Freemasonry — the one dealing with the philosophical, and the other with the historical aspect of the subject — may fairly represent the genius, or the Ideals and aims of Masonry. How far short of this ideal Masonry may fall today, it is no part of the object of this book to show. No one, however, at all familiar with the subject, will for a moment undertake to maintain that nothing is left to be accomplished. It is, indeed, something grand and sublime to have conceived such an ideal, and to have striven in any measure toward its realization; and this, Masonry has done from its earliest history.

There is a thread of tradition connecting modern Masonry with the most ancient Mysteries of Antiquity. The ancient landmarks may be discovered in every nation and time. "Notwithstanding the connection that so evidently exists," says Dr. Rebold, "between the ancient Mysteries and the Freemasonry of our day, the latter should be considered an imitation rather than a continuation of those ancient Mysteries; for initiation into them was the entering of a school, wherein were taught art, science, morals, law, philosophy, philanthropy and the wonders and worship of nature." — Rebold's *History,* p. 62.

The universal Science and the sublime philosophy, once taught in the Greater Mysteries of Egypt, Chaldea, Persia, and India, and among many other nations of antiquity, is a dead letter in modern Freemasonry. The intelligent Mason, however, should be the last person in the world to deny that such wisdom once existed, for the simple reason that the whole superstructure of Masonry is built upon the traditions of its existence, and its ritual serves as its living monument. Proficiency in the preceding degree is everywhere made a reason for advancement in Masonry. This proficiency is made to consist in the ability of the candidate to repeat, word for word, certain rituals and obligations already passed, the meaning or explanations of which constitute the lectures in the various degrees. The usage at this point, in the United States at least, serves rather to secure the rights and benefits of the Lodge to those entitled to them, and to withhold them from all others, than to advance the candidate in real knowledge. In other Masonic jurisdictions, however, a different custom prevails. Of the Belgium Lodges, for example, a Brother writes as follows:

"Our Lodge, called 'La Charite,' at Orient Charlevoi, is under obedience of the great Orient at Brussels, and has the Scottish Rite. No Mason is supposed to know anything of the ritual by heart. Questions and answers are read out, especially at initiation. The work of the Mason is supposed to be interior work in himself, before it can become exterior labor. So in order to obtain his degrees he has to do some work of his own, and no one is supposed to learn anything by heart, except words, signs and passwords. Now I have to tell you that every Mason is supposed to do some literary work on general subjects concerning the welfare of man, human institutions, sociology, history, philosophy, philanthropy, etc., etc., and it is such work that a young Mason is supposed to do. Then, after reading these papers, they are discussed by all the members of the Lodge present, perhaps for three or four meetings, until the subject seems to be exhausted. This develops, in the young Mason, his intelligence and his moral feeling."

As will be shown in a later section, this method conforms to that pursued in the Lesser Mysteries of Antiquity, which were preparatory for the Greater Mysteries.

It should be borne in mind that in modern Freemasonry, in the Ancient Mysteries, and in all of the great Religions, there was always an Exoteric portion given out to the world, to the uninitiated, and an Esoteric portion reserved for the initiate, and revealed by *degrees,* according as the candidate demonstrated his fitness to receive, conceal, and rightly use the knowledge so imparted. Few professed Christians are, perhaps, aware that such was the case with Christianity during the first two or three centuries. The following quotations from Albert Pike's great work may therefore be of interest. On page 541 (*et seq.*) he says:

"This, in its purity, as taught by Christ himself, was the true primitive religion, as communicated by God to the Patriarchs. It is no new religion, but the reproduction of the oldest of all; and its true and perfect morality is the morality of Masonry, as it is the morality of every creed of antiquity."

St. Augustine says:

"What is now called the Christian Religion existed among the ancients, and was not absent from the human race until Christ came, from which time the true religion, which existed already, began to be called Christian." [1]

St. Augustine was Bishop of Hippo, born in 347 A.D., and lived near enough the time of Christ to know whereof he wrote.

But to continue our quotations from *Morals and Dogma*:

"In the early days of Christianity, there was an initiation like those of the Pagans. Persons were admitted on special conditions only. To arrive at a complete knowledge of the doctrine, they had to pass three degrees of instruction. The initiates were consequently divided into three classes: the first, *Auditors;* the second, *Catechumens;* and the third, the *Faithful.* These doctrines, and the celebration of the Holy Sacraments, particularly the Eucharist, were kept with profound secrecy. These Mysteries were divided into three parts: the first styled the Mass of the Catechumens; the second, the Mass of the Faithful. The celebration of the Mysteries of Mythras was also styled a Mass, and the ceremonies used were the same. There were found all the sacraments of the Catholic Church, even the breath of confirmation." ...

"The Basilideans, a sect of Christians that arose soon after the time of the Apostles, practiced the Mysteries with the old Egyptian legend. They symbolized Osiris by the Sun, Isis by the Moon, and Typhon by Scorpio, and wore crystals bearing these emblems, as amulets or talismans, to protect them from danger, upon which were also a brilliant star and the serpent. They were copied from the talismans, of Persia and Arabia, and given to every candidate at his initiation. They all claimed" — (Gnostics, Marcosians, Ophites, etc.) — "to possess a secret doctrine, coming to then directly from Jesus Christ, different from that of the Gospels and Epistles, and superior to those communications, which, in their eyes, were merely exoteric. This secret doctrine they did not communicate to every one; and among the extensive sects of the Basilideans, hardly one in a thousand knew it, as we learn from Irenasus. We know the name of only the highest class of their initiates. They were styled *Elect*, or *Elus*, and 'Strangers to the World.' They had at least three degrees — the Material, the Intellectual, and the Spiritual, and the lesser and greater mysteries; and the number of those who attained the highest degree was quite small."

"In the *Hierarchiae*, attributed to St. Dionysius, the Areopagite, the first Bishop of Athens, the tradition of the sacrament is said to have been divided into three degrees of grades — *Purification, Initiation*, and *Accomplishment or Perfection* — and it mentions also, as part of the ceremony, *the bringing to sight*. The Apostolic Constitutions, attributed to Clemens, Bishop of Rome, describe the early church, and say: 'These regulations must on no account be communicated to all sorts of persons, because of the mysteries contained in them.'"

It is interesting to contrast the utterances of early Bishops of the Christian Church with the Bulls and Anathemas of excommunication of later Popes, hurled against the Masons for entertaining the same doctrines and practicing the same rites. But this was after the idea of dominion had seized the modern church, which tolerates no rival, and would destroy all opposition. Papal supremacy must be maintained at any cost.

Tertullian, who died about a. d. 216, says in his *Apology*:

"None are admitted to the religious mysteries without an oath of secrecy. We appeal to your Thracian and Eleusinian mysteries; and we are specially bound to this caution, because if we prove faithless, we should not only provoke Heaven, but draw upon our heads the utmost rigor of human displeasure."

Clemens, Bishop of Alexandria, born a. d. 191, says, in his *Stromata*, that he can not explain the Mysteries, because he should thereby, according to the old proverb, "put a sword into the hands of a child." He frequently compares the discipline of the Secret with the "Heathen Mysteries as to their internal and recondite wisdom."

Origen, born A.D. 134 or 135, answering Celsus, who had objected that the Christians had a concealed doctrine, said:

"Inasmuch as the essential and important doctrines and principles of Christianity are openly taught, it is foolish to object that there are other things that are recondite; for this is common discipline with that of those philosophers in whose teachings some things were exoteric and some esoteric; and it is enough to say that it was so with some of the disciples of Pythagoras."

The formula which the primitive church pronounced at the moment of celebrating its mysteries, was this: "Depart ye Profane! Let the Catechumens, and those who have not been admitted or initiated, go forth."

Archelaus, Bishop of Cascara in Mesopotamia, who, in the year 278, conducted a controversy with the Manichaeans, said:

"These mysteries the church now communicates to him who has passed through the introductory degree. These are not explained to the Gentiles at all; nor are they taught in the hearing of Catechumens, but much that is spoken is in disguised terms, that the Faithful, who possess the knowledge, may be still more informed, and those who are not acquainted with it may suffer no disadvantage."

Cyril, Bishop of Jerusalem, was born in the year 316 and died in 386. In his Catechesis he says:

"The Lord spake in parables to his hearers in general; but to his disciples he explained in private the parables and allegories which he spoke in public." ... "Just so the church discovers its mysteries to those who have advanced beyond the class of Catechumens: we employ obscure terms with others."

St. Basil, the great Bishop of Caesarea, born in the year 326, and dying in the year 376, says:

"We receive the dogmas transmitted to us by writing, and those which have descended to us from the Apostles, beneath the mystery of oral tradition; for several things have been handed to us without writing, lest the vulgar, too familiar with our dogmas, should lose a due respect for them. This is what the uninitiated are not permitted to contemplate; and how should it ever be proper to write and circulate among the people an account of them."

St. Gregory Nazianzen, Bishop of Constantinople, A.D. 379, says:

"You have heard as much of the mystery as we are allowed to speak openly in the ears of all; the rest will be communicated to you in private; and that you must retain within yourself.'" ... "Our mysteries are not to be made known to strangers."

The foregoing quotations are from Pike's *Morals and Dogma, pp.* 141, 142, 143, 144, and 145. To this list of witnesses are also added St. Ambrose, Archbishop of Milan, a. d. 340; St. Chrysostom of Constantinople (354-417); Cyril of Alexandria, Bishop in 412; Theodoret, Bishop of Cyropolis in Syria in 420, and others to the same effect.

It is beyond controversy, that there was an exoteric and an esoteric doctrine with the early Christians; that the esoteric doctrines were communicated orally in the mysteries of initiation; and that these mysteries conformed to and were originally derived from those of the so-called Pagan world. The Mystery of Christ received a new interpretation after the first Nicene Council, and as the Church sought dominion, it lost the Great Secret, and since then has denied that it ever existed, and done all in its power to obliterate all its records and monuments. While we are concerned with Masonry rather than Christianity, it is, nevertheless, necessary to show the connecting links, in order that the "Ancient Landmarks" may not only be discerned, but correctly interpreted. Neither Christianity nor Freemasonry is the direct and lineal descendant of the Greater Mysteries of Antiquity, but both are imitators, and both have failed to preserve the Key of interpretation, and are generally unaware that such a Key ever existed. My contention is not against either Masonry or Christianity, but for the rejuvenation of both, through the restoration of the Secret Doctrine to each. Modern Masonry never possessed the Key, while many of the early Christian sects had it in their possession, but in time lost it through worldliness, the greed for earthly dominion, and the decay of Spirituality.

Something further may be shown as to the origin of the Christian Mysteries. In the year 525 B.C., Cambyces, called "the mad," led an army into Egypt, overran the country, destroyed its cities, palaces and temples, scattered its priest-initiates, and reduced the country to a Persian province. Many of its priests took refuge in Greece, and conveyed thither the Egyptian Mysteries, which Pythagoras had journeyed to Egypt to obtain half a century earlier. In the time of Plato, a century later, the Mysteries were in a flourishing condition, and in them he learned his sublime philosophy. At the beginning of our era the mysteries had declined. There remained, however, the Gnostics, the Essenes, and the Therapeutae of Alexandria, and from these the Christian mysteries were undoubtedly derived. The Neoplatonists, headed by Ammonius Saccus, undertook to preserve the primitive revelation, and the utterances of the Christian Bishops to which I have referred, show how the Secret Doctrine was ' adopted from the earlier mysteries by the primitive Christians during the first three centuries of our era. After the first Council of Nice, A.D. 325, little more was heard of the earlier doctrines, and with the burning of the Great Library of Alexandria, Catholic supremacy and the dark ages obliterated the primitive wisdom in Western Europe, as it was also overrun by hordes of barbarians from the north. The principal seats of learning were the convents. Coming now to the dawn of the 16th century, and the great Protestant Reformation, we find Johann Trithemius, Abbot of St. Jacob, at Wurtzburg, celebrated as one of the greatest of Alchemists and Adepts; and Cornelius Agrippi and Paracelsus were his pupils. John Reuchlin, a famous Kabalist of that time, and counted as one of the most learned men in his day in Europe, was the friend and perceptor of Luther, and Luther's first public utterances were a course of lectures on the philosophy of Aristotle. A strong effort was made to revive the ancient wisdom, but the age was too gross and superstitious, and the Reformation resulted in centuries of blind belief, and the suppression of the Secret Doctrine.

Modern Freemasonry honors as its ancient great teachers Zoroaster, Pythagoras, Plato, and many others, and in some of its degrees gives a brief summary of their doctrines. Masonry, in a certain sense, includes them all, and has adopted their precepts. They were all initiates in the mysteries, and fundamentally their doctrines were the same. All taught the existence of the G. A. O. U., the immortality of the soul, and the unqualified Brotherhood of Man; and with these primitive and fundamental truths Masonry is in full accord.

The Guilds of Masons, or Builders, with which modern Freemasonry claims connection, doubtless suggested the name of Mason, the symbolism of a Builder, and perhaps the form of organization or advancement by degrees, as Apprentice, Fellowcraft and Master, representing the three degrees of the ancient mysteries.

The past two or three centuries at most will include the whole of the history of modern Freemasonry. The organization is recent, but its principles, when clearly denned, and intelligently interpreted, are eternal, and are in full accord with the greater mysteries of antiquity.

The foregoing running comment on some of the ancient landmarks will enable us to draw comparisons and derive interpretations of Masonic symbols and glyphs from ancient mysteries, and so to discover the science and philosophy that constitute the genius of Masonry. Instead of being an imitation of the Mysteries of Antiquity, Masonry should become their Restoration and Perpetuation through the coming centuries, not by relaxing its discipline? or changing its ritual, but by deepening the learnings intensifying the zeal and elevating the aim of every Brother throughout the world.

[1] Quoted by Heckethorne — "Secret Societies," p. 12, Introduction: "They were first called Christians at Antioch."

Chapter Three - The Genius of Freemasonry

The traditions, glyphs and ritual of Freemasonry cluster around the building of the temple; the legend of the widow's son, Hiram-abiff, who lost his life in the defense of his integrity, and the search for the Lost Word of the Master. As the candidate progresses, degree after degree, he is furnished with the working-tools suited to his degree of knowledge and proficiency, given instruction as to their use; the lesser and greater *lights* are revealed and explained; and through all, each outer form, or material thing, is shown to be a symbol of a deeper mystery, a concealed potency.

This is, in brief, the language and the philosophy of symbolism, or the exoteric and the esoteric garb of Truth. The method itself, outside of all details or applications, has a deeper scientific significance than most persons are aware of. This method of instruction is not fanciful or arbitrary, but conforms to the process, of Eternal Nature in building an atom or a world; a daisy or a man. Cosmos has evolved from Chaos, and yet Chaos remains the Eternal Potency; what Plato called the "*World of Divine Ideas.*" This will be more fully explained in a subsequent chapter. For the present, it may suffice to say, that from primitive space, primordial ether, or what modern science might call the Matrix or origin of the "nebulous mass," the earth and all that it contains has evolved. The essential form, the *idea* of all things; the potency or force; and the matter as we now discern it, must have existed in primordial space. Therefore, these two always exist, viz., the inner potency, and the outer act; the concealed Idea, and the outer form; the inner meaning, and the outer event. Each is in its turn a symbol of the other. Hence the saying on the Smaragdine Tablet, *as above so below.* All outward things are therefore symbols, or embodiments of pre-existing Ideas, and out of this subjective ideal realm all visible things have *emanated.* This doctrine of emanations is the key to the philosophy of Plato, and that of the Gnostic sects from which the early Christians derived their *mysteries.* This fact is mentioned here in order to show the deep foundations of the glyphs of Masonry.

In the Ritual of Masonry, King Solomon's temple is taken as a symbol. The building and the restoration of the temple at Jerusalem are dramatically represented in the work of the Lodge, and in the ceremony of initiation, by a play upon words and parity of events, and applied to the candidate, with admonition, warning or encouragement, as the drama unfolds. The measurements and proportion of the temple are dwelt upon in order to bring in the science of numbers, form, and proportion, so manifest in architecture, and to connect them with the "spiritual temple" with which they all have the same, though less obvious, relations. The symbolism is fitted to ideal relations, rather than to actual existences or historical events. Sol-om-on represents the name of Deity in three languages, and the biblical history is doubtless an allegory or myth of the Sun-god. There is no reliable history of the construction of any such temple at Jerusalem, and recent explorations and measurements have greatly altered the dimensions as heretofore given. Hiram Abiff is dramatically represented to have lost his life when the temple was near completion, and yet it is recorded that after the completion of the temple he labored for years to construct and ornament a palace for the King. Add to these facts the statement that the temple was constructed without the sound of hammer or any tool of iron, and it is thus likened more nearly to that other "*Spiritual Temple,* not made with hands, eternal in the heavens," and the literal and historical features disappear, and the symbolism stands out in bold relief. Masonic Lodges are dedicated to the Sts. John; one of whom, the Evangelist, opens his Gnostic Gospel with the Greek philosophy of the Logos, the principle of emanation already referred to; and the other, the Seer of Patmos, writes a book symbolical of ancient initiations, which many a non-initiate has tried in vain to interpret. It may thus be seen that there is a deep significance in the dedication of Lodges to the Sts. John. Take, for example, Revelations xxi, 16: "And the city lieth foursquare, and the length is as large as the breadth; and he measured the city with the reed, twelve thousand furlongs. The length, and the breadth and the height of it are equal" (a perfect cube). "And he measured the wall thereof, an hundred and forty and four cubits, according to the measure of a man, that is, an angel." The language is evidently a veil, designed to conceal the real meaning from the uninitiated. As the measure of man; that is, a perfect man, or "angel," we have the cube as a symbol of perfect proportion. Hence a *Square Man*. The temple of Sol-om-on; the Cubical City — which unfolded becomes a cross, and hence the "measure of a man" — all these refer to the work of regeneration, or initiation. [1] The rebuilding of the temple after the plan drawn upon the Trestle-board, by which it shall be like that spiritual temple, not made with hands, plainly refers to initiation from which results perfect proportion and perfect harmony. In a later section of this work this mathematical and geometrical basis of virtue and wisdom, or knowledge and power, will be further explained. It is unknown to the Craft of Masonry except in its bare outline and cruder symbolism: it is nowhere hinted that there is an inherent relation and full equivalent between absolute mathematics and spiritual power.

"A very limited knowledge of the history of primitive worship and mysteries is necessary to enable any person to recognize in the master mason, Hiram, the Osiris of the Egyptians, the Mithras of the Persians, the Bacchus of the Greeks, the Atys of the Phrygians, of which these people celebrated the passion, death and resurrection, as Christians celebrate today that of Jesus Christ. Otherwise, this is the eternal and unvarying type of all the religions which have succeeded each other upon the earth. In an astronomical connection, Hiram is the representative of the Sun, the symbol of his apparent progress, which, appearing at the south gate, so to speak, is smote downward and more downward as he advances toward the west, which passing, he is immediately vanquished and put to death by darkness, represented, in following the same allegory, by the spirit of evil; but, returning, he rises again, conqueror and resurrected." [2]

After a long and very learned discussion of the phonetic and philological meaning, use, and derivation of certain god-names, Albert Pike says, page 79:

"Khurum, therefore improperly called *Hiram,* is Khur-om, the same as *Her-ra, Hermes,* and *Her-acles,* the personification of Light and the Sun, the Mediator, Redeemer and Savior."

And, again, page 81, he says:

"It is merely absurd to add the word, *'Abif,'* or *'Abiff,'* as part of the name of the artificer. *Abin* (which we read Abif) means 'of my father's' ... 'formerly one of my father's servants' or 'slaves.'"

As to the Fellowcrafts concerned in the conspiracy, they are shown to have more than one meaning; astronomically this relates to the signs of the Zodiac, the "three wicked ones" representing the winter solstice or death of the year, and consequent subjugation of the Sun-god! Other meanings will be shown further on. "Is it an accidental coincidence," asks Bro. Pike, in *Morals and Dogma,* p. 82, "that in the name of each murderer are the two names of the Good and Evil Deities of the Hebrews; for *Yu-bel* is but *Yehu-bal* or *Yeho-bal;* and that the three final syllables of the names, a, o, m, make A. U. M., the sacred word of the Hindoos, meaning the Triune-God, Life-giving, Life-preserving, Life-destroying" (Brahma, Vishnu, Siva), "represented by the mystic character **Y**."

And, again, on page 620, Bro. Pike says:

"This word could not be pronounced except by the letters; for its pronunciation as one word was said to make Earth tremble and even the angels of Heaven (elementals) to quake with fear."

The aim of the writer at this time is to show the general connection of Masonic glyphs with those of ancient times. The real meaning will appear further on.

As already declared, modern Masonry being but an imitation of ancient genuine Mysteries, the writer has no design of reading into it a meaning which can not be fully verified. For the greater part, modern Masons are dealing with symbols, the Key for the real interpretation of which they never possessed, or even suspected that it existed. It remains for the future to determine whether any considerable number of our Masonic Brethren really desire to possess in fuller measure the Living Truth which the dead-letter text conceals. That Living Truth exists, and is as accessible to every Mason as is the dead-letter or the dumb-show under which it masquerades in every Lodge.

As to the sprig of *Acacia,* Bro. Pike says: "The genuine *Acacia* also is the thorny tamarisk, the same tree which grew up around the body of Osiris. It is a sacred tree among the Arabs, who made of it the Idol Al-Uzza, which Mohammed destroyed. It is abundant as a bush in the desert of Thur, and of it the 'crown of thorns' was composed, which was set on the forehead of Jesus of Nazareth. It is a fit type of immortality on account of its tenacity of life; for it has been known, when planted as a doorpost, to take root and shoot out budding boughs above the threshold."

Here, again, we see a symbol ages old, revived and adopted in many forms, and further, that Immortality was not "brought to light" for the first and only time by the "Man of Sorrows" of the Christians; yet in every case is the symbol none the less true. Whether any of these sun-gods or Redeemers were historical characters or not, the symbolism teaches everywhere the same eternal truths: the Resurrection and the Life; Redemption and Immortality.

After being obligated and brought to light, the candidate in the third degree is bantered with the statement that undoubtedly he now imagines himself a Master Mason. He is informed not only that such is not the case, but that there is no certainty that he ever will become such. He subsequently starts on his Journey for the discovery of the Lost Word. The method by which he undertakes to obtain it, and the names of the three Fellowcrafts already referred to as brothers, have a very deep significance. After many trials, he receives a substitute, which he is to conceal with great fidelity "till future generations shall discover the lost word."

The method by which he receives and is ever to transmit or use even the substitute, is made exact and definite, and guarded by solemn obligations. The meaning of both the great secrecy and the use of the word are left entirely to conjecture, beyond the statement that it is a sacred name, and must never be profaned, or taken in vain, or carelessly used; and I venture the opinion, that not one Mason among ten thousand has ever been able to discover why.

The force of the obligation is therefore in the oath and not in the reason. As a matter of fact, the real reason is scientific to the last analysis; scientific to a degree beyond the penetration, up to the present time, of the "radiant matter" or the *Roentgen Ray* of Modern Science. The *Word* concerns the science of rhythmic vibrations, and is the key to the equilibrium of all forces and to the harmony of Eternal Nature.

This tradition of the *Ineffable Name* is brought into Masonry from the Hebrew Kabalah, and how it became lost is partly historical, at least. The ancient Hebrew Priests evidently undertook to fit to the names of their tribal-deities the symbolism and traditions of the far East. If the Master's Word were really a word at all, the Deity of the Hebrews might perhaps represent it as well as any other. It is a question of phonetics, however, rather than mere orthography. Beneath the Hebrew text of the Pentateuch lies concealed the science of the Kabalah. The Anathemas threatened for him who should alter, by a single letter or "Yod," the outer text, had therefore a deeper meaning. The priests of many nations of antiquity were initiates in the Mysteries, and as such they were Monotheists, while the ignorant masses were idolaters. The monotheism of the Jews was of a robust character, and their priests and prophets had a hard time to preserve their people from the seductive polytheism and abominations of surrounding nations. The Ineffable Name was not only concealed, but "terrible as an army with banners." Jehovah was jealous, revengeful, vindictive toward the evil-doer, and tolerated no rival in the broad expanse of Cosmos. In no religion of antiquity is the anthropomorphic image of Deity so strongly defined, and the Creator of man and worlds made so exceedingly human.

The Kabalah, on the contrary, embodying considerable of the true and ancient Secret Doctrine, held a different idea of Divinity. While carrying the tradition, therefore, of the lost word as the Ineffable Name of Deity, the symbolism was taken as literal fact, and the people who were commanded to "make no graven image" ended by making a gigantic idol, half Moloch and half Man. Amid such contradictions, the symbolism adopted from the purer and gentler Aryans was ill at ease and far from home. Rev. Dr. Garrison claims in a "Contribution to the History of the Lost Word," appended to Foot's *Early History and Antiquities of Freemasonry,* that the four-syllabled name, Jehovah, was held by the Hebrews as the Ineffable, and that *Adonai* was used as a substitute. The Highpriest once every year, at the time of the atonement, entered alone into the Holy of Holies and there repeated the name. The name was thus withdrawn from and finally lost by the common people. This is ingenious and too literal to cover the case. The old query, "What is in a name?" is, after all, not so easy of answer; or the answer might be, "every thing or nothing," according as you understand it or look at it. Before the introduction of the Masoretic points or indices of vowel sounds, the consonants were read by metrically intoning the text. The principle of the Mantram was therefore known to the Highpriest at least, and, therefore, the Word, the Name, that Known in all its plenitude and used with power, "caused the whole world to shake," may have been used or invoked in the Holy of Holies by the Kabalistic Hierophant. Some who read this may be even yet so ignorant of the potency of sound as to smile at the credulity and gullibility that indites it; and yet so superstitious over the *letters of a name* as to believe them more sacred in one form than another! Notwithstanding, it is the letter that killeth, and the Spirit (the breath) that maketh alive. The consonants composing the Hebrew alphabet are about as sacred as so many wooden blocks. If one knows how to arrange the blocks, and endow them with life, so that they may "bud and blossom like Aaron's rod," that of course is a very different matter.

"There are dangers inseparable from Symbolism, which afford an impressive lesson in regard to similar risks attendant on the use of language. The imagination called in to assist the reason usurps its place, or leaves its ally helplessly entangled in its web, Names which stand for things are confounded with them; the means are mistaken for the ends; the instrument of interpretation for the object; and thus symbols come to usurp an independent character as truths and persons. Though perhaps a necessary path, they are a dangerous one, by which to approach the Deity; in which many, says Plutarch, mistaking the sign for the thing signified, fell into a ridiculous superstition, while others, in avoiding one extreme, plunge into the no less hideous gulf of irreligion and impiety." ...

"It is through the mysteries, Cicero says, that we have learned the first principles of life, wherefore the term 'initiation' is used with good reason." ...

"To employ nature's universal symbolism instead of the technicalities of language, rewards the humblest inquirer and discloses its secrets to every one in proportion to his preparatory training to comprehend them. If their philosophical meaning was above the comprehension of some, their moral and political meanings are within the reach of all." ...

"These mystic shows and performances were not the reading of a lecture, but the opening of a problem. Requiring research, they were calculated to arouse the dormant intellect. They implied no hostility to Philosophy, because Philosophy is the great expounder of symbolism." [3]

There is a Grand Science known as Magic, and every real Master is a Magician. Feared by the ignorant, and ridiculed by the "learned" the Divine Science and its Masters have, nevertheless, existed in all ages, and exist today. Masonry in its deeper meaning and recondite mysteries constitutes and possesses this Science, and all genuine Initiation consists in an orderly unfolding of the natural powers of the neophite, so that he shall become the very thing he desires to possess. In seeking Magic, he finally becomes the Majus. All genuine Initiation is, like evolution and regeneration, from within. Devoid of this inner meaning and power, all rituals are but foolish jargon, and all ceremonies an empty farce. Even such the rituals of Masonry have become to many. That the Christ-life and the power that made Jesus to be called *Christos,* Master, whereby he healed the sick, cast out devils, and foretold future events, is the same Life revealed and attained by initiation in the Greater Mysteries of Antiquity, is perfectly plain. The disrepute into which the Divine Science has fallen has arisen from its abuse and degradation.

In the middle ages, and in fact, in every age there have been dabblers in magic; sorcerers and necromancers, who, possessing some of the secrets, and imbued with none of its beneficence, have used their knowledge and power for purely personal and selfish ends. Hypnotism and Phenomenal Spiritualism are sufficient illustrations of the power to which I refer, and the abuse to which it may be put. Magic, *per se,* is always a Science, and up to a certain point it may be cultivated without regard to its use, or the well-being of man; although any abuse of it is fatal to the magician.

The popular idea is that education consists largely in the cultivation of the intellectual powers. An average standard of morals is always recommended by educators, and its outer form is illustrated by religious ceremonies. But intellectual cultivation alone, no matter to what extent it may be carried — and the further it goes in this one-sided way the worse for all concerned — is in no sense an evolution. Perfect intellectual development, without spiritual discernment and moral obligation, is the sign-manual of *Satan.* Intelligence, without goodness, lies athwart the Divine Plan in the evolution of Cosmos. Intellect and Altruism by no means necessarily go hand in hand. One may have a very clear intellect, have quick perceptions, and be a good reasoner, and yet be very wicked. On the other hand, one may be very dull intellectually, and yet be kind, brotherly and sympathetic to the last degree. A world made up of the former would be -a bad place to live in; if of the latter, a thousand times to be preferred. Magic contemplates that all-around development which, liberating the intellect from the dominion of the senses and illuminating the spiritual perceptions, places the individual on the lines of least resistance with the inflexible laws of nature, and he becomes nature's co-worker or hand-maid. To all such, Nature makes obeisance, and delegates her powers, and they become Masters. The real Master conceals his power

43

and uses it only for the good of others. He works "without the hope of fee or reward."

Discerning that knowledge is power, designing and evil men desire to possess both knowledge and power for entirely selfish purposes. It may be readily discerned that the more knowledge and power a purely selfish man possesses, the more inimical to humanity he becomes. He can do less harm if kept in ignorance. This is especially the case in regard to those deeper sciences which deal with mind, and influence the thoughts and actions of others. Suppose one were able to hypnotize large numbers of persons at once, and compel them to do his bidding; and that his motives were not only selfish, but all results injurious to his agents. Such a person would be a Magician, and, as his motive would be purely selfish, a "Black Magician." Modern Science, purely materialistic in its aims and conclusions, has always, till very recently, ridiculed the idea embodied in Magic, and were it not for the fact that it has been compelled to recognize, under the name Hypnotism, since the time of Braid, the very force which it denied and condemned in the days of Mesmer, it might be difficult to find a palpable and undeniable illustration of what kind of power is involved in Magic.

But Hypnotism is not even the alphabet of the vocabulary known to the real Master or Magician. It is but an empirical dabbling in a power of gigantic proportions, the key to which makes of its possessor either a Savior or a Destroyer of his fellowmen.

We have only to reflect on the use already made of Hypnotism for public exhibitions, for personal greed, by its "Professors" — God save the mark — to determine whether any larger output of Occult knowledge would be desirable or beneficial to mankind at large.

The traditional-Lost Word of the Master is a key to all the science of Magic. The knowledge of the Master is not empirical. It does not consist of a few isolated formulae by which certain startling or unusual effects can be produced. The Magician's art is based on a science far more deep and exact than modern physical science has yet dreamed of, and back of this science lies a philosophy as boundless as Cosmos, as inexhaustible as Time, and as beneficent as the "Father in Heaven." If the Masonic meaning of *Master: Perfect and Sublime Master: Prince Adept:* etc., is less than I have indicated, then it is a roaring farce, or a stupendous humbug. The conception of Masonry is true, but it has adopted or imitated the ritual and glyphs of a science, the key to which not one Mason in ten thousand possesses, and hence the tradition of the Lost Word has a literal, no less than a symbolical meaning. The "Substitute" is given to the neophite — "till future generations shall find the True Word." The question now propounded to every "obligated," or so-called Master Mason, is — is the present 'the generation in which that which was lost shall be found? and each must answer for himself singly; just as he entered his lodge, first saw the light, and took his obligation; just as every real Master, or "White Adept," has done since the beginning of time. There exists in Masonic literature many learned essays on the history, orthography and philology of the *Lost Word;* but I am acquainted with no treatise that apprehends the nature of the real secret like that of Brother Albert Pike in his great work, and yet, if he knew the whole secret, he concealed it at last.

The more immediate source from which the legend is imported into Masonry is the Jewish Kabalah, derived doubtless from the Chaldean and Zoroasterian form of the Secret Doctrine; the principles and methods of which were unfolded by the late lamented Bro. J. Ralston Skinner, A. & A. S. R. 32 . Bro. Skinner's greater works, however, aside from his *Source of Measures,* and a large number of pamphlets, exist only in Manuscript, and are of so abstruse a character as to be of little use except to profound scholars. Running all through the Talmud are found references to the Secret Wisdom, while the *Sohar,* the *Kabalah Denudata,* and other Kabalistic works are all written with a veil designed to conceal the secret from the uninitiated, and to be meaningless without the key. Bro. Skinner's discoveries were the reward of genius, made as the result of stumbling on one of the keys that "unlock the Golden Gates of the Palace of the King." His discoveries lay the foundation for a systematic and scientific study of the Kabalistic form of the Secret Doctrine which lies concealed beneath the Hebrew text of the Pentateuch, and which no commentary has ever revealed or intended to reveal. Perhaps another generation of biblical Hebrew Scholars may discard their preconceptions, prejudices and superstitions of the mere verbiage of the text sufficiently to desire to discover the real meaning of the Pentateuch, as to the creation of Men and Worlds. Copies of Bro. Skinner's unpublished researches have been so placed by his special desire and act, that they may be preserved for such future investigators and not again be lost to the world.

But the Hebrew Kabalah is but one of many sources from which the Secret Science may be derived, and it is not the one which in its form of Symbolism and method of interpretation is best fitted to the present age. When the symbolism of the Kabalah is read by the key furnished by Bro. Skinner, it requires to be again translated into modern ideas or forms of thought. The basis of it was the *Chaldean Book of Numbers,* no genuine copy of which, if in existence, is accessible to modern students. Several spurious copies are known to exist, and it is possible that a genuine copy may be produced at the proper time. For be it remembered that Genuine Masters, "Prince Adept Masons," have always existed, and no book or record worth preserving or necessary for the good of man is ever lost. In secret crypts, alike inaccessible to the vandal hand of man, and the corrosion of time and decay, these treasures are said to be preserved.

All human progress runs in cycles. Modern materialistic science has had its brief day, and Philosophy has already undermined its foundations. The new age will show a genuine revival of Philosophy.

The immortal principles enunciated by Plato, clothed in modern garb of thought, less involved and dialectical, will again command the attention of the thinking world. Every one is aware that the source of Plato's knowledge was the Mysteries; he was an Initiate, and on almost every page reveals the obligation he is Under not to betray to the common people the secrets taught only to initiates under the pledge of secrecy.

The foregoing digression seemed necessary in order to show the real basis for the traditions of the Lost Word, and to put beyond cavil, at least with the more rational, the idea that the Master's Word is a real thing, the genuineness and power of which is not overdrawn in the parables and glyphs of Freemasonry.

"The True Word of a Mason is to be found in the concealed and profound meaning of the *Ineffable Name of Deity* communicated by God to Moses" (rather by the Priests of Egypt. — B.), "and which meaning was long lost by the very precautions taken to conceal it. The true pronunciation of that name was in truth a secret, in which, however, was involved the far more profound secret of its meaning." ...

"Thus the Ineffable Name not only embodies the great Philosophical Idea, that the Deity is the *Ens,* the *To On,* the absolute Existence, that of which the Essence is To Exist, the only Substance of Spinoza, the *Being,* that never could not have existed, as contra-distinguished from that which only becomes; not Nature or the Soul of Nature, but that which created Nature; but also the idea of the Male and Female Principles, in its highest and most profound sense: to wit, that God originally comprehended in Himself all that is; that matter was not co-existent with Him or independent of Him; that He did not merely fashion and shape a pre-existing chaos into a universe; but that *His Thought* manifested itself outwardly in that universe, which so became, and before was not, except as comprehended in Him; that the Generative Power, or Spirit, and the Productive Matter, ever among the ancients deemed the Female, originally were in God, and that He Was and Is all that Was, that Is, and that Shall be; in whom all else lives, moves, and has its being." "This was the great Mystery of the Ineffable Name, ...and of course its true pronunciation and its meaning became lost to all except the select few to whom it was confided; it being concealed from the common people, because the Deity, thus metaphysically named, was not that personal and capricious, and, as it were, tangible God in whom they believed, and who alone was within reach of their rude capacities...This was the profound truth hidden in the ancient allegory and covered from the general view with a double veil. This was the exoteric meaning of the generation and production of the Indian, Chaldean, and Phoenician Cosmogonies; of the Active and Passive Powers; of the Male and Female Principles; of Heaven and its Luminaries generating, and the Earth producing; all hidden from vulgar view, as above its comprehension; the doctrine that matter is not eternal, but that God was the only original Existence, the Absolute, from Whom everything has proceeded, and to Whom all returns...And this True Word is with entire accuracy said to have been lost, because its meaning was lost even among the Hebrews, although we still find the name (its real meaning unsuspected) in the Hu of the Druids and Fo-Hi of the Chinese." [4]

"There is in nature one most potent force, by means whereof a single man, who could possess himself of it, and should know how to direct it, could revolutionize and change the face of the world.

"This force was known to the ancients. It is a universal agent, whose supreme law is equilibrium; and whereby, if science can but learn how to control it, it will be possible to change the order of the Seasons; to produce in night the phenomena of day; to send a thought in an instant round the world; to heal or slay at a distance; to give our words universal success, and make them reverberate everywhere." This agent, partially revealed by the blind guesses of Mesmer, is precisely what the Adepts of the middle ages called "elementary matter of the great work." [5] And this is the force of the Keely Motor, and the Frohat of the Secret Doctrine. But to continue our quotations:

"There is a Life-Principle of the world, a universal agent, wherein are two natures and a double current of love and wrath. This ambient fluid pervades everything. It is a ray detached from the glory of the Sun, and fixed by the weight of the atmosphere and the central attraction. It is the body of the Holy Spirit, the Universal Agent, the Serpent devouring his own tail." (See the Seal of the T. S.)

"With this electro-magnetic ether, this vital and luminous caloric, the ancients and the alchemists were familiar. Of this agent that phase of modern ignorance termed physical science talks incoherently, knowing naught of it save its effects; and theology might apply to it all its pretended definitions of spirit."

"Quiescent, it is appreciable by no human sense; disturbed, or in movement, none can explain its mode of action (except a real Master), and to term it a 'fluid' and speak of its 'currents,' is but to veil a profound ignorance under a cloud of words." [6]

"The Kabalah alone consecrates the alliance of the Universal Reason and Divine Word; it establishes, by the counterpoise of two forces apparently opposite, the eternal balance of being; it alone reconciles Reason with Faith, Power with Liberty, Science with Mystery; it has the keys of the Present, the Past, and the Future."

"The Bible, with all the allegories it contains, expresses, in an incomplete and veiled manner only, the religious science of the Hebrews. The doctrine of Moses and the prophets, identical at bottom with that of the ancient Egyptians, also had its outward meaning and its veils. The Hebrew books were written only to recall to memory the traditions; and they were written in Symbols unintelligible to the Profane. The Pentateuch and the prophetic poems were merely elementary books of doctrine, morals or liturgy; and the true secret and traditional philosophy was only written afterward, under a veil still less transparent. Thus was a second Bible born, unknown to, or rather uncomprehended by, the Christians'" (of later times), "a collection, they say, of monstrous absurdities; a monument, the adept says, wherein is everything that the genius of philosophy and that of religion have ever formed or imagined of the Sublime; a treasure surrounded by thorns; a diamond concealed in a rough dark stone."

"One is filled with admiration on penetrating into the Sanctuary of the Kabalah, at seeing a doctrine so logical, so simple and at the same time so absolute. The necessary union of ideas and signs, the consecration of the most fundamental realities by the primitive characters; the Trinity of Words, Letters and Numbers; a philosophy simple as the alphabet, profound and infinite as the World; Theorems more complete and luminous than those of Pythagoras; a theology summed up by counting on one's fingers; an Infinite which can be held in the hollow of an infant's hand; ten ciphers and twenty-two letters, a triangle, a square and a circle — these are all the elements of Kabalah. These are the elementary principles of the written Word, reflection of that spoken Word that created the world." [7]

And so we might go on quoting from this real "Master of the Veils," this genuine Prince Adept among Masons, whose great work, even as a compilation, is a monument more enduring than brass, and more honorable than the crown of kings. If he did not comprehend to the last veil all that he transcribed — and he too used veils — he discerned enough to teach him how to find the whole. It may thus be seen that the Holy Bible as one of the Great Lights in Masonry has a very profound meaning when coupled with the tradition of the Ineffable Name, or Lost Word. The object set before the neophite in his search for the Lost Word, is, that he may travel in foreign countries and receive Master's wages. [8] This glyph in its outer form is taken from the guilds of practical Masons of two or three centuries ago. The laws then governing the Mark of a Fellowcraft or a Master Builder were very strict, and the Mark was never bestowed unworthily, and when received was a passport among builders over a wide domain. But in a deeper, or Kabalistic sense, the Master's Word, which entitled its possessor to Master's wages, was a very different thing indeed. The wages of the real Master were the satisfaction and the power that flow from the possession of real knowledge. Knowledge is power only when one comprehends that which he possesses, and is, therefore, enabled to use it for the purposes that lie nearest his heart. Bro. Pike shows conclusively that the power of the *Word* lies in the knowledge of the Philosophy which is its perfect synthesis. This is, in part, the meaning of "knowing how to pronounce the Word."

As already stated, the Kabalah of the ancient Hebrews, which Moses derived by initiation into the mysteries of Egypt and Persia, and which Pike and many others declare was identical among the Hebrews, the Egyptians, Hindus and other nations of antiquity, was known as the *Secret Doctrine*. The reason for such a name is fully revealed in what has been shown hitherto. What Pike says regarding the relation of the Pentateuch to the Kabalah, is true of the exoteric scriptures of every nation of antiquity.

How many generations of imbeciles or materialists, think you, my Brother, would it require to recover it? The great majority of mankind in every age not only do not possess the secret and the power of the Master's Word, but are incapable of comprehending it. We do not know a thing because we are told that it is so. Let the gods shout the truth of all the ages into the ears of a fool forever, and still forever the fool would be joined to his folly. Here lies the conception and the principle of all initiations. It is knowledge unfolded by degrees in an orderly, systematic manner, step by step, as the capacity to apprehend opens in the neophite. The result is not a possession, but a growth, an evolution. Knowledge is not a mere sum in addition; something added to something that already exists; but rather such a progressive change or transformation of the original structure as to make of it at every step a New Being. Real Knowledge, or the growth of Wisdom in man, is an Eternal Becoming; a progressive transformation into the likeness of the Supernal Goodness and the Supreme Power.

Initiation and Regeneration are synonymous terms.

The ritual of Freemasonry is based on this natural law, and the ceremony of initiation illustrates, at every step, this principle, and if the result attained 'is a possession rather than a regeneration, in the great majority of cases, the principle remains none the less true. The mere inculcation of moral principles, or lessons in ethics, and their symbolic illustration and dramatic representation, are by no means in vain. These appeal to the conscience and moral sense in every man, and no man has ever been made worse by the Lessons of the Lodge. By these "rites and benefits" the Freemason is, above all men, in our so-called Modern Civilization, the nearest to the Ancient Wisdom. He has possession of the territory in which lie concealed the Crown Jewels of Wisdom. He may content himself, if he will, by merely turning over the sod and gathering only a crop of husks or stubble. He may dig deeper and find not only the Keystone of the Arch, the Ark of the Covenant, the Scroll or the Law, but, using the spirit concealed in the wings of the Cherubim, he may rise untrammeled by the rubbish of the temple, and, meeting *Alohim* face to face, learn also to say *I am that I am!* Does this read like a rhapsody, and are the Landmarks, traditions, and glyphs of Freemasonry nothing more?

The real temple referred to from first to last in Masonry, as in all ancient initiations, is the Tabernacle of the Human Soul.

It is built, indeed, without the sound of hammer or any tool of iron. It is like (made in the likeness of) that other, spiritual temple, not made with hands, eternal in the heavens; for the old philosophy (Kabalah) teaches that the Immortal Spirit of man is the artificer of the body and its source of life; that it does not so much enter in, as overshadow man, while the Soul, the immediate vehicle of the Spirit, inhabits the body, and is dissipated at death. The Spirit is Immortal, pure, and forever undefiled. It is *Christos,* or *Hiram,* the Mediator between the Soul, or physical man, and the Universal Spirit — the Father in Heaven. The "poor, blind candidate," that is, the man of sense, immersed in matter, would learn the *Ineffable Name,* and obtain the Lost Word, and, seeking a short cut, "climbs up some other way." He would have wisdom without self-conquest, power without sacrifice. He will not listen to the voice of pleading, "Be patient, my brother, and when the temple is completed, if found worthy, you shall receive that for which you have so long wrought." No! he will have it now! and he silences the pleading voice, and, defeating only himself, flees into the deserts of remorse and calls upon the rocks to hide him from the pursuit of his accusing conscience. Hiram (Christos) is resurrected. Being immortal, he can not really die. No sin of man is final. Realizing his error and purified by suffering, the spirit in man being again lifted up, even defeat gives promise of victory, and he receives a Substitute for the Lost Word. He hears, however faint or dim, the Divine Harmony. Future generations, that is, further trials and more sincere endeavor, promise greater reward. He learns to "know, to will, to dare, and to keep silent." Brotherly love, Relief and Truth; Prudence, Fortitude, Justice and Mercy — all the Virtues and all the Beatitudes are inculcated.

The candidate is taught, not merely to tolerate another's religion, but to respect it as his own; though still adhering to that into which he was born. To make reasonable this obligation, he is shown through the Kabalah or Secret Doctrine that at the heart of every great religion lie the same eternal truths.

Forms and observances only differ. *The Ineffable Name* is spelled in many ways, yet the Word is one and eternal. Masonry is not only a universal science, but a world-wide religion, and owes allegiance to no one creed, and can adopt no sectarian dogma, as such, without ceasing thereby to be Masonic. Drawn from the Kabalah, and taking the Jewish or Christian verbiage or symbols, it but discerns in them universal truths, which it recognizes in all other religions. Many degrees have been Christianized only to perish; as every degree eventually will if circumscribed by narrow creeds, and dwarfed to the bigoted apprehension, so as to exclude good men of any other communion. Is Jesus any the less *Christos,* because Christna was called "the Good Shepherd"? or because the Mexican Christ was crucified between two thieves? or because Hiram was three days in a grave before he was resurrected? Are we not as selfish in our religion as in our other possessions? Then why is man, while cherishing as his most sacred possession, the religion of his fathers, eternally seeking to degrade and destroy that of his brother?

The Great Republic, to which Bro. Pike refers, is the Ideal of Masonry; the Genius that hovers like a protecting angel over the Lodge. Make it impossible for a Jew or Parsee, Buddhist or Brahmin, to enter any Lodge without witnessing the profanation of his sacred altars or contempt for his religion, and the angel hides her face and retreats from altars already profaned by unbrotherliness. Masonry is the Universal Religion only because, and only so long as, it embraces all religions. For this reason, and this alone, it is universal and eternal. Neither persecution nor misrepresentation can ever destroy it. It may find no place in a generation of bigots; it may retire for a century; but again comes a Master Builder with the Key to the "Shut Palace of the King," throws open the blinds, lets in the light, kindles anew the fire on the sacred altar, clears away the rubbish, when behold! the tessellated pavement is as bright as when it first came from the quarries of truth, the jewels are of pure gold and brighten at the touch, and the great lights are undimmed and undecayed. "When the candidate is ready the Master appears." And yet men are so foolish and so vile as to imagine that they can destroy this heirloom of the ages; this heritage from the Immortals! No age is so dark as to quench entirely the light of the Lodge; no persecution so bloody as to blot out its votaries; no anathemas of Popes so lasting as to count one second on its Dial of Time! These, one and all, serve only to keep the people in darkness, and retard the reign of Universal Brotherhood. Therefore for humanity — the Great Orphan — the real Master laments. He smiles at the passions of Popes or Kings and pities the folly of man. He *only waits* indifferent as to results, knowing these to be under eternal law; but ready and willing, whenever and wherever the instruction entering the listening ear may find lodgment in the faithful breast. For ages Kings, Popes and Synods have done their best to kill this Secret Doctrine by anathematizing or burning its Masters. The Jesuits got possession of its Lodges, transformed out of all recognition many of its degrees, and made of them an abject tool of the Sacerdotal hierarchy.

But at last the Jesuits became glutted with gold and impudent with power, and the Church became frightened and destroyed or banished the destroyers. Will power in high places ever desist or relax its warfare? Never! It can, however, be forever ignored or defied; but it will never allow its secrets to be laid bare, and a greater to stand in its place. He who anticipates such beneficence has read history in vain. The Kingdom of Heaven is taken by force, but it is moral force, or moral courage, and the first great battle is for the conquest of self; the subjugation of that time-serving spirit, which, joined to the idols of the flesh, is blind to the truths of the eternal spirit. He who conquers here may at last become *Master*.

[1] See Plate XIII.
[2] Reybold's "History of Freemasonry." Note by Translator, p. 392.
[3] Morals and Dogma, p. 64.
[4] Morals and Dogma, p. 700 *et seq.*
[5] Morals and Dogma, p. 734.
[6] Morals and Dogma, p. 734.
[7] Morals and Dogma, p. 475.
[8] The wages of a *real* Master is *Knowledge* and *Power* to travel where he will in space.

Chapter Four - The Secret Doctrine

"The true Mason is a practical Philosopher who, under religious emblems, in all ages adopted bywisdom, builds upon plans traced by nature and reason the moral edifice of Knowledge." [1] "As Grand Master of all Symbolic Lodges, it is your especial duty to aid in restoring Masonry to its primitive purity." [2]

"Among all the ancient nations there was one faith and one idea of Deity for the enlightened, intelligent, and educated, and another for the common people. To this rule the Hebrews were no exception." [3] "It (Masonry) is philosophical, because it teaches the great Truths concerning the nature and existence of one Supreme Deity, and the existence and immortality of the soul." [4] "The Universe, which is the uttered Word of God, is infinite in extent. There is no empty space beyond creation on any side. The Universe, which is the Thought of God pronounced, never was not since God never was inert." [5]

"I, Myself, never was not, nor thou, nor all the Princes of the Earth; nor shall we ever hereafter cease to be." [6]

"Every thing emanates from a Single Principle and a primitive Love, which is the Moving Power of All, and governs all."

"Masonry teaches and has preserved in its purity the cardinal tenets of the old primitive faith, which underlie and are the foundation of all religions." [7]

There is no fact in history more easily and completely demonstrable than the existence of the Secret Doctrine in all ages among all people, and of Adepts or Masters who were familiar with its teachings, and were more or less capable of expounding its principles.

It is equally demonstrable that this Secret Doctrine was the real foundation of every great Religion known to man; that only the initiated Priest or Hierophant knew the real doctrines in any case, and only these, as a rule, in the earliest history of each religion.

Furthermore, the Sacred Books of all religions, including those of the Jews and the Christians, were and are no more than parables and allegories of the real Secret Doctrine, transcribed for the ignorant and superstitious masses. All commentaries written on these Sacred Books, whether on those of Moses, the Psalms and the Prophets of Judaism, the Gospels of the Gnostics and Christians, or those written on the Sacred Books of the East — the Vedas, Puranas, and Upanishads — all either make confusion more confounded when written by one ignorant of the Secret Doctrine, or, when written by initiates, but ring the changes on, or further elaborate the parables and allegories.

It is, furthermore, easily demonstrable that the Secret Doctrine came originally from the far East, and is the Primitive Wisdom Religion. Its earlier records are now found in India and Thibet; thence it seems to have traveled to Ethiopia; thence to Egypt and Chaldea. This route, or order of transmission, however, is not to be easily ascertained with accuracy, nor is it a matter of any consequence to us at the present time. It is everywhere and at all times essentially the same; only the outer gloss, the parables and allegories concealing it differ among different people.

Underlying this Secret Doctrine was a profound philosophy of the creation or evolution of worlds and of man. The present humanity, in many quarters of the globe, has evolved on the intellectual plane so far that there now exist a very large number of persons capable of apprehending this old philosophy, and, at the same time, capable of understanding the responsibility incurred in misusing or misinterpreting it. A large number of persons have reached, on the intellectual plane, the state of manhood; and are capable of partaking of the "fruit of the tree of knowledge of Good and Evil." There is, therefore, no reason why this old philosophy should be longer concealed. On the other hand, there are reasons why it should be known. Empirical knowledge has advanced in certain directions into the realm of Psychism, and the arts anciently designated by the term *Magic,* and it is imperative that the dangers that attend these pursuits should be pointed out and demonstrated, in order that they may be avoided by the beneficent, and that the ignorant or innocent may be afforded protection. How far these modern inroads into Occultism or ancient Magic extended very few persons seem to realize. It is therefore high time that the philosophy of the East should illumine the science of the West, and thus give the death blow to that intellectual diabolism, and spiritual nihilism, known as Materialism, and this only the Secret Doctrine can accomplish. Grave responsibility, however, is incurred by such a revelation. Those who, like the professional Hypnotists and the Vivisectionists, have sinned, perhaps ignorantly, and thus have been unconsciously "Black Magicians," will eventually find no avenue of escape. Ignorance can no longer cover their inhuman or cruel practices. The Hypnotist can not reduce the mind of a trusting but ignorant brother to the condition of imbecility, without facing the law that counts such a crime as no less than murder. The new Science, resulting from the union to which I have referred, and which, I believe, Mr. J. M. Rusk proposes to call Psycho-Physics, will be well understood before the close of the 20th century, and many an old score in the intellectual arena will be settled.

They know little of the forces at work, or the principles involved, who imagine that there is sufficient force in dissolving creeds, or in the dying throes of materialism, to greatly retard the progress of these truths by sneers or ridicule, or to prevent their triumph by any opposition they can bring to bear against them. They have waited for millenniums, *and their time has come.*

"To recapitulate; the Secret Doctrine was the universally diffused religion of the ancient and prehistoric world. Proof of its diffusion, authentic records of its history, a complete chain of documents, showing its character and presence in every land, together with the teaching of all its great Adepts, exist to this day in the secret crypts of libraries belonging to the Occult Fraternity." As to the danger of revealing these doctrines to the profane:

"The danger was this: Doctrines such as the planetary chain, or the seven races, at once give a clue to the seven-fold nature of man. For each principle is correlated to a plane, a planet, and a race; and the human principles are, on every plane, correlated to sevenfold occult forces [8] — those of the highest planes being of tremendous power." "No one styling himself a 'scholar,' in whatever department of exact science, will be permitted to regard these teachings seriously. They will be derided and rejected, *a priori*, in this century; but only in this one. For in the 20th century of our era scholars will begin to recognize that the Secret Doctrine has neither been invented nor exaggerated, but, on the contrary, simply outlined; and finally, that its teachings antedate the Vedas." And in a footnote it .is said: "This is no pretension to prophesy, but simply a statement based on the knowledge of facts."

In speaking of the source from which the present version of the Secret Doctrine is derived, our author says, regarding an "old book": "So very old that our modern antiquarians might ponder over its pages an indefinite time, and still not quite agree as to the nature of the fabric upon which it is written...The most ancient Hebrew document of occult learning, the *Siphrah Dzeniouta,* was compiled from it, and that at a time when the former was already considered in the light of a literary relic."

"The days of Constantine were the last turning point in history. The period of the Supreme struggle that ended in the Western world throttling the old religions in favor of the new ones, built on their bodies. From thence the vista into the far distant Past, beyond the 'Deluge' and the 'Garden of Eden,' began to be forcibly and relentlessly closed by every fair and unfair means against the indiscreet gaze of posterity. Every issue was blocked up, every record that hands could be laid upon, destroyed." [9]

This same Constantine who, with his soldiers environed the Bishops at the first Council of Nice, A.D. 325, and dictated terms to their deliberations, applied for initiation into the Mysteries, and was told by the officiating priest that no purgation could free him from the crime of putting his wife to death, or from his many perjuries and murders. Every careful and unbiased student of history knows why the Secret Doctrine has been heard of so little since the days of Constantine. An exoteric religion and belief in a personal God blotted it out for self-protection; and yet, oh, irony of history! the very Pentateuch conceals it, and for many a student of Kabalah of the coming century the seals will be broken.

In trying to apprehend an outline, at least, of the Secret Doctrine, two ideas should be kept constantly in mind, viz., Space and Consciousness; the former, in relation to all that is either thought or asserted regarding Nature and Deity; and the latter, in regard to Deity, Nature, and Man. In the last analysis, both Space and Consciousness elude us. What they are, *per se,* we shall never know. We may as well take them as facts in our experience, and in analyzing that experience, both Consciousness and Knowledge will expand.

"What is that which was, is, and will be, whether there is a Universe or not: whether there be Gods or none? asks the Senzar Catechism. And the answer made is — Space."

Now space is not Nature, nor is it Deity. Space may be said to contain nature or creation, and to conceal Divinity. It is therefore the point of emanation and the vanishing point.

The Occult Catechism contains the following questions and answers:

"What is it that ever is?" "Space, the eternal Anupadaka" (parentless). "What is it that ever was?" "The germ in the Root." "What is it that is ever coming and going?" "The Great Breath." "Then there are three eternals?" "No, the three are one." "That which ever is, is one; that which ever was, is one; that which is ever being, and becoming, is also one: and this is Space."

"For clearer understanding on the part of the general reader, it must be stated that the Occult Science recognizes Seven Cosmical Elements — four entirely physical, and the fifth (Ether) semi-material, as it will become visible in the air toward the end of the Fourth Round, to reign supreme over the others during the whole of the Fifth. The remaining two are as yet absolutely beyond the range of human perception. These latter will, however, appear as presentiments during the 6th and 7th Rounds respectively. These seven elements, with their numberless Sub-Elements (far more numerous than those known to Science), are simply conditional modifications and aspects of the one and only Element. This latter is not Ether, nor even Akasa, but the Source of these. The Fifth Element, now advocated quite freely by Science, is not the Ether hypothesized by Sir Isaac Newton — although he calls it by that name, having associated it in his mind, probably, with the Aether, 'Father-Mother' oi Antiquity. As Newton intuitionally says: 'Nature is a perfect circulatory worker, generating fluids out of solids, fixed things out of volatile, and volatile out of fixed. Subtle out of gross, and gross out of subtle.' ...Thus, perhaps, may all things be originated from Ether." (*Hypoth.* I, 675.) [10]

It is interesting to notice, in this connection, that Newton was familiar with the writings of Jacob Boehmen, the "Teutonic Theosopher," and that among Newton's posthumous papers were found copious notes and translations from his works. As to the "Races," referred to in the above quotation, it need only be said in passing, that the Secret Doctrine declares that in the evolution of humanity there are to be seven Races, of which ours is now the fifth, and that each race makes seven rounds on our planetary chain, of which rounds the present race is now in the fourth, with here and there a "fifth rounder" appearing. The Secret Doctrine teaches, not only the immortality of the soul, but the perfectibility of humanity by orderly evolution on this Earth. This doctrine concerns the general evolution which the present work touches only incidentally; it is complicated, and necessarily so.

There are three fundamental propositions that underlie the Secret Doctrine, (*a*) "An Omnipresent, Eternal, Boundless, and Immutable Principle on which all speculation is impossible, since it transcends the power of human conception, and could only be dwarfed by any human expression or similitude. It is beyond the range and reach of human thought — in the words of Mandukya, "unthinkable and unspeakable." This Infinite and Eternal Cause

— dimly formulated in the "Unconscious" and "Unknowable" of current European philosophy — is the rootless root of "all that was, is, or ever shall be." ...In Sanscrit it is "Sat." This "Beness" is symbolized in the Secret Doctrine under two aspects.

On the one hand, Absolute abstract Space, representing bare subjectivity, the one thing which no human mind can either exclude from any conception or conceive of by itself.

On the other, Absolute abstract Motion representing "Unconditioned Consciousness." "Spirit (or Consciousness) and Matter are, however, to be regarded, not as independent realities, but as the two facets or aspects of the Absolute, which constitutes the basis of conditioned Being whether subjective or objective." "Considering this metaphysical triad" (the only reality, Spirit and Matter) "as the Root from which proceeds all manifestation, the 'Great Breath' assumes the character of precosmic Ideation." (Plato's *World of Divine Ideas.*)

"It is the *fons et origo* of force and of all individual consciousness, and supplies the guiding intelligence in the vast scheme of Cosmic Evolution. On the other hand, precosmic root-substance (Mulaprakriti) is that aspect of the Absolute which underlies all the objective planes in Nature."

(b) The second of the three postulates of the Secret Doctrine is: "The Eternity of the Universe *in toto* as a boundless plane: periodically 'the playground of numberless Universes incessantly manifesting and disappearing,' called 'the manifesting stars' and the 'sparks of Eternity,' 'The Eternity of the Pilgrim' (the Monad or Self in man) is like a wink of the Eye of Self-Existence. 'The appearance and disappearance of Worlds is like a regular tidal ebb of flux and reflux.'"

The third postulate is:— (c) "The fundamental identity of all Souls with the Universal Over-Soul, the latter being itself an aspect of the* Unknown Root; and the obligatory pilgrimage for every Soul — a spark of the former — through the Cycle of Incarnation (or Necessity) in accordance with Cyclic and Karmic law, during the whole term." ... "The pivotal doctrine of the Eastern philosophy admits no privileges or special gifts in man, save those won by his own Ego through personal effort and merit throughout a long series of Metempsychosis and Reincarnations." [11]

Every soul must "work out its own salvation," and "take the Kingdom of Heaven by force." Salvation by faith and the vicarious atonement were not taught, as now interpreted, by Jesus, nor are these doctrines taught in the exoteric Scriptures. They are later and ignorant perversions of the original doctrines. In the Early Church, as in the Secret Doctrine, there was not one Christ for the whole world, but a *potential* Christ in every man. Theologians first made a fetish of the Impersonal, Omnipresent Divinity; and then tore the *Christos* from the hearts of all humanity in order to deify Jesus; that they might have a God-man peculiarly their own!

All the ancient Mysteries had the true doctrine, and the early Christians had it. Masonry, uncontaminated by the disciples of Loyola, had and has it also.

The one Immutable Principle, referred to in the first proposition (*a*), is called in the Kabalah, Ain Soph: the word Ain meaning "nothing." This is not Jehovah, or Adonia, or the G,A,O,U; for it is not .itself creative, but the *cause* of Creation. ("Causeless Cause.")

The Jewish "creators" (plural) are the *Elohim;* the "Principalities and Powers." In this conception of Divinity lies the secret of the Ineffable *Name, i.e.,* the Nameless. The Lost Word is to the Master who possesses it and knows how to "pronounce" it, what the Logos or creative power is to the Nameless. Hence the real Master creates, and in this sense is a god. This will be further shown in connection with the Seven Principles and the Nature of Man.

The second proposition — the Eternity of the Universe *in toto* — reveals the law of cycles and the "incessant" work of creation.

In other words, the creative process never had a beginning, and will never have an end. There is one endless succession of Universes. Worlds and Solar systems continually appear and disappear.

Each sun, star, or solar system has a period of activity and a period of repose; emanates from, and is drawn back into, the All and the One. These periods are called the "Nights and days of Brahm,"

The idea that a God with human qualities and human passions made the Earth out of nothing in six days of twenty-four hours each, is sufficiently miraculous, and sufficiently childish, for those who are ready to burn all who do not accept their interpretation.

To endow a God with the power of performing the impossible and the inconceivable, was considered sufficient honor bestowed.

The law of periodicity is a necessary corollary of the order of events and the flight of time. Rythmical, orderly, harmonious movements in space give us our conception of time, as how fast, how often, how slow, how regular, etc. The ear is a time organ, and the basic property of the Ether is Sound. This idea of periodicity, or law of cycles, is symbolized in Freemasonry in many ways.

In the three, five, or seven years of pilgrimage or penance; in the seven years of plenty, and seven of famine. "In the low twelve" and "the high twelve," in calling the Craft from labor to refreshment, and many others. In the third postulate we have "the fundamental identity of all souls with the One," which gives the basis of the eternal and universal Brotherhood of Man, and the basis of the entire scheme of human Evolution.

When these doctrines are clearly understood, they will be seen to go far beyond any modern scheme of evolution, though running on somewhat similar lines. In them the entire scheme of Cosmic and human evolution will be found to have been worked out ages ago. Pythagoras and Plato found these doctrines completely unfolded in the Mysteries. Brother Pike says repeatedly that they have been far oftener disfigured than apprehended, and never transcended in modern times. Masonry derives its genius, its inspiration, its glyphs, and its traditions from this philosophy as taught in the Mysteries. How short-sighted and time-serving, then, must it be for Masonry to allow its Grand Traditions, its priceless inheritance to be dwarfed and overlaid by illogical interpretations, derived from records that were in the beginning, and before being disfigured* by ignorance or cupidity, only an allegory of the true doctrines, prepared by "those who knew" for the ignorant masses, who demanded a sign and could never rise above a fetish. This is like bartering a magnificent diamond for a lump of common clay. Shall Masons now complete the folly by trying to convince themselves and others that the clay is the only diamond?

How much one's idea of God colors all his thoughts and deeds is seldom realized. The ordinary crude and ignorant conception of a personal God more often results in slavish fear on the one hand, and Atheism on the other. It is what Carlyle calls "an absentee God, doing nothing since the six days of creation, but sitting on the outside and seeing it go!" This idea of God carries with it, of course, the idea of creation, as something already completed in time; when the fact is that creation is a process without beginning or end. The world — all worlds — are being "created" today as much as at any period in the past. Even the apparent destruction of worlds is a creative, or evolutionary process. Emanating from the bosom of the All, and running their cyclic course; day alternating with night, on the outer physical plane, they are again *indrawn* to the invisible plane, only to reemerge after a longer night and start again on a higher cycle of evolution. Theologians have tried in vain to attach the idea of *immanence* to that of personality, and ended in a jargon of words and utter confusion of ideas. A personal Absolute is not, except in potency. God does not *think,* but is the *cause* of Thought. God does not love, he is Love, in the perfect or absolute sense; and so with all the Divine Attributes. God is thus the concealed Logos, the "Causeless Cause," the "Rootless Root." God never manifests Himself (to be seen of men). Creation is His manifestation: and as creation is not complete, and never will be, and as it never had a beginning, there is a concealed or unrevealed potency back of and beyond all creation, which is still God. Now, Space is the most perfect symbol of this *idea* of Divinity; for it enters into all our concepts, and is the basis of all our experiences. We can not fathom it, or define it, or exclude it from a single thought or experience. Space is boundless, infinite, unfathomable, unknowable: in all, over all, through all. We know that It Is: and that is all we know about It.

But are not these just the attributes that are assigned to the Absolute and Infinite Deity? and they are all *negations.* God, says the Kabalah, is *No Thing.* But the Theologian will hasten to say that this is pure Pantheism. It is no more Pantheism than it is Atheism, for, as already shown, the Ain Soph is before and beyond Creation or Cosmos. It is not God deduced or derived from Nature, but precisely the reverse; nature derived from God, and yet God remains "the same, yesterday, today, and forever" — the Changeless. The stability of nature is derived from the unchangeableness of God. God never tires, is not exhausted at His work, needing rest. That were so human as to be childish, and the idea, perhaps, originated from the cyclic law found in the Kabalah of the "Days and Nights of Brahm," the "Manvantaras and Pralayas," or periods of "outbreaking" and of "inbreathing" in the cycles of evolution.

Hence the parable, given to the ignorant or the profane, of God's working and then resting. If the reader will but reflect a moment on his own process of breathing, he will find that the inbreathing (inhalation) and the outbreathing (exhalation) are equal, and equally active processes, although so different, each being the opposite of the other: each, in its turn, the cause of the other. Stop one, and the other ceases also. The more one reflects on this symbol of the *Great Breath* which creation is, the more will he understand of both Eternal Nature and his own being.

But it may be asked: is man to be deprived of all idea of Personality except his own? By no means. God is the Author of Being, is the Author of Personality. He personifies Himself, *i.e.,* expresses that potency of Himself which personality is, through Man. The Hand of Providence is always a human hand. Humanity is both the vehicle and the agent of what man has called the Providence of God.

Humanity *in toto*, then, is the only Personal God; and *Christos* is the realization, or perfection of this Divine *Persona,* in Individual conscious experience. When this perfection is realized, the state is called *Christos,* with the Greeks, and *Buddha,* with the Hindoos. Hence the Christ is at-one with the Father. "Be ye perfect, even as your Father in Heaven is perfect."

Humanity *in toto!* What is it? Is it the generations of the present age? or of any age in the past? or of the future? and these alone? Justice rules the Universe, and is the foundation of all Law. Justice is the "Kingdom," the "Permanency" of Deity. Humanity, therefore, means *every human being ever born, in any age, or to be born in coming ages, on this Planet*. All are "in the Hollow of His hand." One God, One Law for all! else there is no Justice.

And if:t shall be done unto each according to the deeds done in the body; if as a man soweth so shall he reap, the only logical deduction is Law governing action and determining results according to Absolute Justice. And this the Kabalah, the Secret Doctrine and Masonry, and all Sacred Books, and all Religions, everywhere teach. By taking the Symbols for the thing symbolized, men have made contradictions out of details, and then built up a system of final rewards and punishments, attaching to acts in time; and claimed their *unreason* and *injustice* as binding to all eternity. The result "is Atheism and Materialism; for there is an instinct in man, as part of his Divine inheritance, and that instinct is an innate sense of Justice. Destroy this, and the result is Atheism, pure and simple. Destruction of the sense of Justice has honeycombed the churches, and been the parent of modern Materialism. It is true that Materialism is not the logical, but the actual result. The issue is not logically between an Unjust God and no God, but between a God that is inconceivable because Unjust; and a God that is conceivable because Just, and therefore the issue of the Supreme Reason.

But this philosophical concept of Divinity has another and still wider bearing. It concerns not only man's personal life, but determines his relations to his fellow men. It is the basis of ethics, and furthermore co-ordinates all his experience and all his knowledge, and this leads to true wisdom. "To know God is the Supreme Wisdom."

It will be urged by modern Theologians that this view dethrones Christ. To this objection the answer is that any other view orphans Humanity. It is far more important that men should strive to become Christs than that they should believe that Jesus was Christ. If the Christ-state can be attained by but one human being during the whole evolution of the race, then the evolution of man is a farce and human perfection an impossibility.

Jesus is no less Divine because all men may reach the same Divine perfection. Again, it will be urged, "There is no other name given under Heaven or amongst men whereby ye can be saved." But this is the Ineffable Name, which every Master is to possess and become, and salvation and perfection are synonymous. It has also been shown that every act in the drama of the life of Jesus, and every quality assigned to Christ, is to be found in the life of Krishna and in the legend of all the Sun-Gods from the remotest antiquity.

That which the orthodox Christian will find to oppose to this view is not that it dethrones or degrades Christ, but that it disproves the idea of Christ as their exclusive possession, and denies that all other religions are less Divine than their own. We have brought the same selfishness into our religions that we indulge in regard to our other possessions, such as wife and children, and houses and land, and country; and the same partisan spirit as in our politics, and this more than anything else appears to justify selfishness in general, militates against the Brotherhood of Man, and prevents the founding of the "Great Republic, composed of many Nations and all people." This idea of Universal Brotherhood which was a cardinal doctrine in the Ancient Mysteries — as it is involved in the first postulate of the Secret Doctrine, and openly declared in the third; and which is equally given the very first rank in Masonry — is the logical deduction from our idea of Divinity, and of the essential nature and meaning of *Christos.* Humanity, *in toto,* as already explained, is the personification of the Divine in Creation, and the idea of exact and universal Justice regards each individual of all the myriads constituting Humanity with equal favor. There are no favorites in the Divine Conception, Justice of God toward all implies Justice toward each other amongst men. This principle of Justice is Law Universal, and this principle of Brotherhood and the perfectibility of man's nature through evolution necessitate Reincarnation. The number of souls constituting Humanity, though practically innumerable, is, nevertheless definite. Hence the doctrine of pre-existence taught in all the Mysteries applies to "every child of woman born;" all conditions in each life being determined by previous living. This will be further elaborated in another section of this work. Thus the Fatherhood of God in the Personification of Divinity in Humanity includes the Universal and Unqualified Brotherhood of Man.

The real Masters in all ages, knowing this from the lessons taught in the mysteries of initiation, have ever been the foes of Autocrats, Oligarchies, and Oppression in every form, whether Ecclesiastical or Political. Masons are taught to obey the laws of the country in which they reside. They are not agents of Revolution, but of Evolution. By enlightenment and persuasion they may strive to reform a nation or a church. The true Republic is the outgrowth of Brotherhood, and a jealous monarch in Church or State will naturally oppose the diffusion of doctrines that tend to the liberation and the enlightenment of the people.

It is true, however, that all the Masters or Adepts may not be equally enlightened or equally prudent.

Mystics like Jacob Boehmen, or Adepts like St. Germain, or Masons like de Molai, or Philosophers like Bruno, or other Agents of the Great Lodge sought only to instruct and enlighten mankind.

The rabble were deaf to their doctrines and appeals, and turned like ravenous wolves upon them.

"Because true Masonry unemasculated, bore the banners of Freedom and Equal Right, and was in rebellion against spiritual tyranny, its Lodges were proscribed in 1738 by an edict of the States of Holland. In 1737 Louis XV. forbade them in France. In 1738 Pope Clement XII. issued against them his famous Bull of Excommunication, which was renewed by Benedict XIV.; and in 1743 the Council of Berne also proscribed them." [12]

"Masonry has ever the most vivid remembrance of the terrible and artificial torments that were used to put down new forms of religion, or extinguish the old. It sees with the eye of memory the ruthless extermination of all the people of all ages and both sexes because it was their misfortune not to know the God of the Hebrews, or to worship Him under the wrong name by the savage troops of Moses and Joshua. It sees the thumb-screws and the racks, the whip, the gallows, and the stake, the victims of Diocletian and Alva, the miserable Covenanters, the Non-Conformists, Servetus burned, and the unoffending Quaker hung. It sees the persecutions of Peter and Paul, the martyrdom of Stephen, the trials of Ignatius, Polycarp, Justin and Irenaeus; and then, in turn, the sufferings of wretched Pagans under the Christian Emperors, as of Papists in Ireland under Elizabeth, and the bloated Henry; the Roman Virgin naked before the hungry lions, young Margaret Graham tied to a stake at low-water mark, and there left to drown, singing hymns to God until the savage waters broke over her head; and all that in all ages have suffered by hunger and nakedness, peril and prison, the rack, the stake, the sword — it sees them all, and shudders at the long roll of human atrocities. And it sees the oppression still practiced in the name of religion — men shot in a Christian Jail in Christian Italy for reading the Christian Bible; in almost every Christian State laws forbidding freedom of speech on matters relating to Christianity, and the gallows reaching its arm over the pulpit."

"The fires of Moloch in Syria, the harsh mutilations in the name of Astarte, Cybele, and Jehovah; the barbarities of imperial Pagan Torturers; the still grosser torments which Roman Gothic Christians in Italy and Spain heaped on their brother-men; the fiendish cruelties to which Switzerland and France, the Netherlands, England, Scotland, Ireland, America, have been witness, are' none too powerful to warn man of the unspeakable evils which follow from mistakes and errors in the matter of religion, and especially from investing the God of Love with the cruel and vindictive passions of erring humanity, and making blood to have a sweet savor in his nostrils, and groans of agony to be delicious in his ears."

"Man never had the right to usurp the unexercised prerogative of God, and condemn and punish another for his belief." [13]

All men are brothers by all the laws of Nature and by the very Being of God. But so long as Religion defines Heresy as a crime, or imagines a God with human attributes, "man's inhumanity to man" will continue to make "countless millions mourn," and find vent for all evil passions justified by their idea of God. But, some will say this is all a thing of the past. Mankind, especially in Christian countries, have outgrown these relics of Barbarism. Alas! if it were only true. We do not drown, or burn, or torture physically, but quite as subtle torture to the sensitive is found in scorn, contempt, ridicule, and ostracism, in slander and defamation of character. Are we any nearer genuine brotherhood today than we were a century ago? or have, we but refined our cruelties and merely disguised the claw of the tiger? Do not supreme selfishness and relentless greed lie at the heart of competition? Are not the Trade Unions and the Syndicates glowering at each other like cages of wild beasts? Ah, my Brother, we are but little removed from Barbarism after all, and it does make all the difference in the world what idea we entertain of God, and what is our basis of Ethics. The one idea of the modern Scheme of Salvation is self-preservation. We must be saved, if all the rest are damned, and competition, and egotism, and selfishness in every form are the legitimate result.

Masonry does not preach a new religion, it but reiterates the New Commandment announced by Jesus, which was also announced by every great reformer of religion since history began. Drop the theological barnacles from the Religion of Jesus, as taught by Him, and by the Essenes and Gnostics of the first centuries, and it becomes Masonry. Masonry in its purity, derived as it is from the old Hebrew Kabalah as part of the Great Universal Wisdom-Religion of remotest Antiquity, stands squarely for the Unqualified and Universal Brotherhood of Man, in all time and in every age. To Christianize Masonry, or to narrow it to the sectarian bounds of any Creed, is not only to dwarf and belittle it, but must inevitably result, as among warring sects, has always resulted with religions, in setting brother against brother, and Lodge against Lodge, and result in final dissolution. This is one of the plainest meanings of the Legend of the Lost Word.

The thinnest veil over the sublime Mystery of the Ineffable Name is Brotherhood and Love! This is the Light of the Logos.

The gross darkness that hangs like a black veil over the *Shekinah* is Selfishness and Hate. Even so hath it ever been; and so will it ever be till Brotherly Love, Relief, and Truth reign universally in the hearts of all Humanity. The refinements of so-called Civilization do not change the essential nature of man. Beneath all these there sleeps or wakes a demon or an angel, and one of these is ever in chains, for no man can serve two masters.

[1] Morals and Dogma, p. 268.
[2] Ibid.
[3] Ibid. 303.
[4] Ibid. 221.
[5] Morals and dogma, p. 206.
[6] Bhagaradgita.
[7] Ibid. 324.

[8] Experimenters with the "Roentgen Ray" may profitably take notice.
[9] Secret Doctrine.
[10] Secret Doctrine.
[11] Secret Doctrine, Introduction.
[12] Morals and Dogma, p. 50.
[13] Morals and Dogma, p. 162 *et seq.*

Chapter Five - The Secret Doctrine (Continued)

Science and Religion

The Science and the Religion (Theology) of the West are in perpetual conflict. The genius of this religion discerns Faith and Miracle as its foundation. Science holds as its ideals Fact and Law. This religion is necessarily illogical, while science is materialistic, and, thanks to both, mankind is as far from any real knowledge of the nature and destiny of the soul as it was a thousand years ago. This conflict has long been maintained; it is a war to the death; both religion and science are being reformed, and long before the battle ceases, neither of the original champions will be found to exist, except in their progeny of doubtful extraction or foreign parentage.

A reconciliation has sometimes been dreamed of, but placed a long way off. The theory or "working hypothesis" of Science is mechanical to the last degree. Matter, Force, Motion, and Law without an underlying Intelligence. Matter is said to be essentially dead and inert, and Mind is regarded as the fortuitous result of combination and aggregation, known as "organization." Evolution is regarded as the result of modification and improvement by use and selection, and the increment carried forward by heredity. In other words, of Autonomy.

The theory of Religion is that of a Personal God and an arbitrary and equally mechanical, though miraculous, creation; of a Revelation equally miraculous; of souls created as by arbitrary caprice of Deity, with the accidental cooperation of man, even in violation of Divine Law. It talks of Laws, but admits their abrogation through the Will (caprice) of God. It is true that neither Science nor Religion has openly formulated the foregoing creeds, but they are fair deductions from the postulates assumed, the logical results of a Nature without Intelligence; and a God who creates Laws only to annul them at His own good pleasure! Reconciliation between Science and Religion thus becomes impossible, because each is a contradiction to itself.

But a reconciliation was reached in the Secret Doctrine ages ago.

The old universal Wisdom Religion was scientific to the last degree; for beneath both Science and Religion was the Philosophy which discerned the orderly processes of Eternal Nature, with no "missing links" in Evolution, and no caprice or contradictions anywhere in Cosmos.

The First Postulate of the Secret Doctrine, already referred to, lays the sure foundation of this old Philosophy.

An Omnipotent, Eternal, Boundless, and Immutable Principle, co-evil and co-extensive with Space: in All, through All, and over All: Divinity Immanent in Nature: Alike the Eternal Cause and Result, each without beginning or end, and each alternating forever!

Law in Nature is the Permanency, the Unchangeableness of the Divine Being. Intelligence in Nature is the Harmony of the Divine Order. Hence, the "Kingdom," the "Foundation," the "Crown," the "Beauty," etc., of the Kabalistic Sephira, or Divine Attributes of Ain Soph, the Boundless. The doctrine of Emanation, taught by Plato and held by the Gnostics and the early Christians, gave the key to cosmic and human evolution. Plotinus said: "God is not the principle of Beings, but the Principle of Principles." Universal Substance, Universal Energy* Universal Law, Universal Life, Universal Intelligence are all emanations or manifestations of the One Principle.

This is not Pantheism, but pure and unadulterated Theism.

The All is One, and that One is Divinity. Spinoza came, perhaps, as near the truth as any one since the days of the old Initiates.

Every atom of matter as every "spot" in space is full of Divinity.

There is neither time nor place where He ("It") is not. The Priest-Initiates among the Hebrews knew this doctrine, as they had it from Old Egypt ("Moses was skilled in all the wisdom of the Egyptians"), and neither Jehovah nor Adonai was the Nameless or the Boundless.

Here, in the First Postulate, lies the complete reconciliation of Science and Religion. Through the Divine Immanence in Nature, and within all, Space concealed, every atom of matter is endowed with Life and Intelligence and bound by Law. Evolution is a Formation, Transformation, and Re-formation, in endless succession, with the outposts of Creation continually drawn upward toward the center in Divinity. Or, Space Involves Divinity, and Evolves Cosmos. At the center of every atom or Sun lies Divinity (Unity); at the circumference unfolds Nature (Diversity); and these two are forever One and at-one.

How any rational mind can fail to see in this philosophy a complete Reconciliation of Religion and Science, it is difficult to understand.

In the beginning, when the world emanates, or begins to manifest visibly, space becomes turgid (called "curds" in the old Hindoo Cosmology) with substance. The invisible becomes visible. This is the first "Matter," and it is called Akasa. On the force side, coincident with this turgescence (prior to "nebula") "Absolute Abstract Motion, representing Unconditioned Consciousness," one of the two *aspects* of Beness — latent potential energy becomes active. Latent Consciousness becomes Cosmic Ideation. This primal energy is called Fohat, "the mysterious link between Mind and Matter, the animating principle electrifying every atom into life." We have now Matter, Force and Motion, with Law as the Guiding intelligence (active) and Consciousness (latent) as Cosmic Ideation, unfolding the Plan; and all these in perfect concord evolving the Symphony of Creation. Of course this Cosmogenesis can be here but roughly outlined.

We have then Akasa, as the Universal Substance, and Fohat, as the Universal Energy, with Intelligence guiding them, Consciousness back of them, and the Roots of all in the Concealed Ain-Soph, the Unknowable. Professor Crooks has taken a long stride in this direction in his metaphysical excursion in search of the "Origin of the Elements," and in his postulation of *Protyle.* He has further touched the septenary key in the order of the emanation of the so-called elements known to modern science. It would be impossible in a work such as this, and equally out of place, to undertake to trace the process running through millions of years by which a planet is evolved; how the turgescence gives rise to denser substance, "set on fire" by friction (Fohat), and how the "Fire-Mist" cools and hardens into Matter on our plane. Though apparent Chaos, here is Cosmos, order and formation, as much as now may be discerned in this present state of our Earth. The real Chaos is Space, which is but latent, potential Cosmos, or Creation asleep. Tracing this process of world-building from the "beginning," the One (negative), abstract Space and absolute Abstract Motion (the *Ineffable Name,* or Deity, lying still back of these, "Nameless" and never manifesting), now become *active,* and here lies the first "Manifestation," a duality: "Father-Mother;" Spirit and Matter; Consciousness and Intelligence. From a latent or potential duality, space and motion, there arises an active manifested duality. Taking latency as the One, the First Logos, we have thus the first Triad, or the "Second Logos." As differentiation goes on the first Triad becomes the Modulus. Fohat "lights the fires," sets the "wheels" (atoms) in motion, and Cosmic Ideation (latent Consciousness becoming active) now gives form to evolving substance. Symbolize this and we have the first triad reflecting itself in matter a double triangle, [1] or a perfect square, with the Ineffable Name *inscribed in the first triangle;* [2] which with the three reflected, making six, and the Name added making the First Septenary. This is the keynote of all that follows; the pitch, the rhythm, and the harmony of Creation: The first octave in the song of the Morning

Stars. The first septenary in the Universal Spectrum of Color: and the first expression of the form into which Matter is molded. To synthesize all these movements in one word we have Fohat as the agent; and *Vibration* as the manifestation. The Master who knows the pitch, quality and amplitude of this first vibration, who can produce this first septenary of sound, color, and form, can by so doing raise his Consciousness to that first or seventh (according as -we count from above downward or the reverse) plane. Such a one knows how to *pronounce* the *Ineffable Name.* It is not only a matter of pure science, dealing with laws of rhythm; a fact, and not a tradition or a sentiment, but it implies absolute At-One-Ment in knowledge and power between all that goes to make up what we call man and all that we call Nature. It is the consummation of human evolution. Hence said the Christ: "It is finished." In giving himself to the world the perfect at-one-ment was attained. In the ethical sense, that is, on the plane of relations of man to man, the *Word* is Renunciation, or self-sacrifice. In the Hindoo tradition regarding the Master's Word there are seven ways of pronouncing it, each involving a different potency and a different result. The Voice of the Silence says:

"Before thou set'st thy foot upon the ladder's upper rung, the ladder of the mystic sounds, thou hast to hear the voice of thy inner God (the Higher Self) in seven manners.

"The first is like the nightingale's sweet voice chanting a song of parting to its mate.

"The second comes as the sound of a silver cymbal of the Dhyanis, awakening the twinkling stars.

"The next is as the plaint melodious of the ocean sprite imprisoned in a shell.

"And this is followed by the chant of Vina.

"The fifth like the sound of bamboo-flute shrills in thine ear.

"It changes next to a trumpet blast.

"The last vibrates like the dull rumbling of a thunder-cloud.

"The seventh swallows all the other sounds. They die, and then are heard no more.

"When the six are slain and at the Master's feet are laid, then is the pupil merged into the one, becomes the one and lives therein."

While these descriptions are of symbols of sounds, they nevertheless represent definite vibrations in the Ether or Akasa, and he who can induce them in himself, can raise his consciousness plane after plane to the seventh, and become at-one with the All. If one has ever fainted or taken an anaesthetic, and remembers the rushing sound that precedes the silence, when consciousness ceases on the outer plane, he has a fact in his own experience giving him the key to *Samadhi.* If he can produce the same condition in himself without fainting or chloroform, for example, but by a knowledge of the laws of vibration, then is he an Adept, and has, and knows how to pronounce the Master's Word.

The "designs on the Trestle-board for the building of the Temple" are the laws that determine the evolution of the Higher Self in Man: while the execution of the plan, or the construction of the temple, in accordance with the plan, means a transformation of the earthly tabernacle — the lower nature — into a likeness with "that other, spiritual temple, not made with hands, eternal in the heavens."

This is again symbolized by the triangle within the square.

The triangle in the square symbolizes potential Being before evolution: Man in the Garden of Eden. The square in the triangle symbolizes regeneration; the purification of the lower earthly nature so that it may "ascend to the Father;" return to Paradise. This is symbolized by the careful position of the compass and square in relation to the Holy Bible, while the three Greater lights, and three Lesser lights again make a double triangle; one greater because above, one lesser because below, which every Mason will understand.

A few years ago these explanations would have seemed to the great majority of persons purely fanciful. But since the recent progress in electricity and photography; since thought and emotion, like light and shade, have been photographed by light emanating from the human body directed by the human Will, the philosophical synthesis of the forces in man is the next step in the search of science for the mystery of man.

It is precisely this synthesis which Masonry possesses in its Symbolism, and we can only read the one by the light of the other, and check both by facts derived by experiments as science advances.

Passing now from these broader metaphysical aspects to the complex nature of man, and we have also the key to his entire nature and evolution.

We begin with the fact of consciousness. Man is not merely a bundle of organs or faculties: he is essentially one. What else can be the meaning of the phrase "Made in the image of God"?

Man is the image, God the reality. Divinity posits a center of consciousness and this evolves into man. Just as in Cosmogenesis, latent consciousness as abstract absolute motion, became with abstract space the Cosmic duality. We speak of this center of consciousness in man as a "spark of Divinity." What Divinity is to Cosmos this spark is to man. Concealed, never manifesting itself, but giving rise to all manifestations in man, it is the apex of the triangle, while Life and Thought are the other two angles.

Starting, then, with this metaphysical concept, we have the Divine Ego, the Higher Self; a metaphysical abstraction, it is .true, like the zero in mathematics, or like Motion and Space, yet the cause lying back of all phenomena, the potency of all actuality.

This is the Ego, the Thinker, the "I am I" in man. So far, it is not conscious, but consciousness; or the cause of it in man's complex nature. It is the "All-seeing Eye." It is Christos, potentially. It is Conscience; the "Sun of Righteousness," in man's world of being. It attaches to the body and the lower life through mind, of which it is the potency, but not the act; the Thinker, but not the Thought.

Mind is the immediate vehicle of consciousness, as matter is called the vehicle of Force.

Thus, from the three postulates of the Secret Doctrine we have, first: Divinity, and Nature at one; second, we have Spirit and Substance as the dual principle from which all Force and all Matter proceed; third, Religion and Science, are consistent, each with itself, and in perfect harmony with each other; fourth, we have a philosophy of the origin, nature, and destiny of Man, agreeing with, and fortified by all previous concepts. The First Postulate teaches the origin and essential nature of all things. The Second Postulate teaches the Law of Cycles, and the process of world-building. The Third Postulate teaches, in harmony with the First and Second, the "fundamental identity" of all souls with the Universal Over-Soul; Brotherhood and the Laws of Karma and Reincarnation, which are the factors in Human Evolution.

Going back, now, to the First Postulate, we find One Principle with whatever "aspects" or "manifestations" the human mind may conceive, and all things, all principles, potencies, powers, derived' from or manifestations of this One: whether it be Matter or Spirit; man or beast; angel or worm; *every thing* from the One; and, after all manifestation, as before, the One is concealed; inexhaustible, unknowable. We know and can know only Its garment, Its manifestations.

Man is called the Microcosm, or little world. The One is in him, as in Nature, the cause of his Being; and as in the Macrocosm, or great world, the One manifests as the many by an orderly descent or differentiation, so in man, from the one principle we have first a triad, and then a quaternary. The three evolve four, making seven. Then from the first seven, "seven times seven," making the "49 fires" [3] of the older Hindu philosophy. Before the reader declares this conception to be altogether fanciful, let him turn to the investigations of modern physical science regarding Color and Sound. Helmholtz estimated that between the highest rate of vibrations giving rise to sound waves apprehensible to the human ear, and the lowest vibration of Light, giving rise to the red of the Solar Spectrum, there would intervene about thirty-four octaves of consonant or dissonant vibrations; and unless there are great gaps in nature, these thirty-four octaves are concerned in producing the phenomena of Nature. It has, furthermore, been demonstrated that there is an exact equation between color and sound vibrations; and that colors have their complementary tones, and tones their complementary colors. In other words, we may see sounds and hear colors.

The modern theory (very old) of the Correlation and Conservation of Force, designates the various forces, as "Special Modes of Motion:" that is, definite vibrations. All colors, sounds, and forms in nature, are the result of definite vibrations. Matter exists on different planes, having different densities, different atomic or molecular structure, and hence different vibrations.

Change the plane, or rather transfer matter from one plane to another, and you change the inherent or normal vibration. Reverse the process, and change by any means the vibration, and you transfer the matter involved to another plane. We must go further. Observation and experiment have shown that as to these various planes we have not a single form of matter, with a single form of vibration, but every plane is complex and compound. All the colors of the spectrum, and all the tones in a musical scale, are resolvable into consonant series of octaves (septenaries). Hence on all the planes above referred to, there is an interpenetration of planes and vibrations.

On each plane there is a dominant chord to which all vibrations conform. Just as we may have in an octave or throughout a symphony a dominant chord. The order of this interpenetration, however, is from above downward. The higher penetrate the lower, while the lower are only latent in the higher. Take, for example, seven planes of which the highest (seventh) represents spirit, and the lowest matter or physical substance. The first or lowest plane is altogether illusory. It has no permanent or real existence. It is not only in continual motion and continual change (Formation, Dissolution, and Reformation) but these are its characteristics. Under certain conditions it disappears (dissolves) from the 1st plane entirely, and passes to the 2d, and to the 3d, 4th, and so on. The greatest activity is on the higher planes, and is greatest on the highest; till all merge in, or return to, the *One,* and Changeless, from which they emanated. All known phenomena in nature testify to the existence of such a law. Hence the saying in the old philosophy: "Nature prefers that matter shall be eternal on the higher planes only."

The grossest physical substance, therefore, is penetrated or saturated with all the higher substances and energies. These are held to subordinate positions by the dominant chord, which is, say, "F," and so are latent or active as the theme unfolds, or as the combination varies. Can any one imagine such a complicated condition and such coordinate results as all the time occur, and yet believe that there is no absolute law governing the whole process? It is not difficult in a general way to formulate the law.

Take the first or lowest plane. It is penetrated by matter of plane No. 2, the next higher. Let us say that each plane represents matter and force, the Cosmic duality. The so-called Force, of plane 1, is the so-called substance of plane 2. But plane 2 is in its turn saturated by the substance and energy of plane 3. Hence the force or energy of plane 2 is the substance of plane 3, while the Force side of plane 3 is latent on plane 2, but active on plane 3. The law, therefore, may be thus formulated: From highest to lowest, the lower is the vehicle (Upadhi) of the higher; and each plane in the ascending order derives its Force or Energy from the Substance of the next higher. In the last analysis, where all are merged in the one, Substance and Energy are seen to be but two aspects of the One Eternal Principle; the "Father-Mother" of the old philosophy.

Passing now from these general considerations to the organic nature of man, and applying these universal laws to his physical, sensuous, intellectual, moral, and spiritual nature, we shall, find that they shed a flood of light on the problem of his nature, origin and destiny.

It is well to bear in mind that our *idea* of God, and our theory of Religion (theology) were the starting points in this philosophy. To deny the existence of God, or to conceive one as illogical, unjust, capricious, personal, and endowed with all human infirmities, equally lead to confusion, ignorance and discouragement, if not to despair.

This philosophy, here but crudely outlined, is not only the foundation of all the sacred books of all religions, but, while it was in them concealed beneath parable and allegory, in the Mysteries of each religion it was taught openly, and constituted the theoretical part of the genuine Initiations. Before undertaking to show how far this philosophy is embodied in the symbols of Masonry, in the Building of the Temple, and the Legend of Hiram, it will be necessary to further unfold the teaching in regard to the complex nature of man.

Man may be viewed from two standpoints: as a concrete whole (an Individual, a conscious unit), and as an aggregate of organs and faculties. Anatomically, man is composed of fluids, tissues, and organs. The fluids are resolvable into inorganic and organic compounds, and resolvable again into elements. The tissues and organs originate from cells, these from molecules, and these again are supposed to be composed of atoms or so-called elements. Physiology classifies the functions of man as organic — mere association of tissues endowed with life like the plant, hence sometimes called vegetative functions: as Animal — viewed from the sensuous plane, and common to all animal life: as Intellectual, in which are generally included the Moral and the Spiritual. Consciousness is usually regarded as incidental, according as it appears or disappears on the physical plane. It has already been shown that in the Secret Doctrine, Consciousness is regarded as the permanent or basic factor in Man's Being. It is never destroyed, never suspended, but may retire from one plane to another. In this sense it may be withdrawn from the physical plane. This old theory of the Ego, or Thinker, and its planes of consciousness on any of which it may be latent or active during its connection with the body, makes it possible or thinkable that the Ego may, in its states of consciousness, transcend the limits of the physical body altogether, and furnishes a conception of the nature and existence of the human Soul. These elements of truth, be it observed, are derived from the phenomena and experiences of the Ego in the physical body, and the key to the problem lies in the planes of Consciousness. It is because modern materialistic science has overlooked the importance, and failed to understand the philosophy of Consciousness, that it denies or is agnostic regarding the existence of the soul. It should also be observed, that we do not put forth a theory of Consciousness as a working hypothesis, but start with Consciousness as an empirical fact in all human experience. Regarding the nature of consciousness itself, we are agnostic enough to suit the Spencers and Huxleys of Science, for we have posited it as the highest point in the nature of man; a "spark" from the Unknowable; the "forever Concealed."

As to changes in states and extension of the bounds of consciousness, this has already been proved empirically in the experiments in hypnotism. Beyond the field of touch, outside the range of sight or sound, as applied to the ordinary functions of the senses, Hypnotic Subjects have been influenced by the silent will, and become conscious of the unexpressed thought of the Hypnotizer. Thus, even modern materialism with its mechanical working hypothesis has worked up to the problem of consciousness.

Had anything been wanting in -this direction, the clues, at least, have been furnished by the experiments in Psychic photography of Dr. Baraduc, reported in the French Academy of Medicine, and many other experimenters are working on the same lines. If the reports are true, Dr. Baraduc has proved by photography the existence of the *Mayavi-Rupa,* the thought-body known to many Adepts of antiquity. Long before this, Mr. J. M. Rusk, of McConnelsville, Ohio, photographed a "thought form" by the light resulting from a strong concentration of the Will. Instances might be multiplied, but enough evidence has already been adduced to give the death-blow to Mechanico-materialistic hypotheses of modern science, and to open the door for the Psychic Science of the East.

Now, the Anatomy and Physiology to which I have referred, offer a certain method of investigating man, and while this method has given rise to magnificent results, it is not, by any means, the only one, nor the most fruitful for all purposes.

The Planes in Nature and in Man, to which I have referred, and the septenary principle in their divisions and relations, offer another method of investigation.

[1] In the Kabalah the "Ancient of Days;" the "Aged of the Aged;" "The Face reflected in the Waters." Akasa is also called "the pure waters of space."
[2] See Plate I.
[3] See Plates I and II.

Chapter Six - The Secret Doctrine (Continued)

The Septenary Nature of Man

We may speak of Life, of Will, of Desire, and of Love as Principles manifesting in Nature and recognized by results. In themselves they may have no definite form, yet are they none the less potent. These principles may take the form of the body of man, as water takes the form of the vessel that contains it, which, if congealed, retains the form of the vessel. Still it is true that water as a body has no definite form of its own. So it is with the principles we are considering. They are metaphysical concepts, not tangible things, but they are causes that lead to tangible results.

It has already been stated that each principle is correlated to a plane, a planet, and a race; and that the human principles are, on every plane, correlated to sevenfold occult forces. It has already been shown how the substances of different planes interpenetrate with the "dominant chord" determining the vibration on any plane. As to the general method of evolution in man, or the relation of Anthropogenesis to Cosmogenesis, it may here be noted that in the various processes of "cooling and hardening," by which the Earth has reached its present state from the "Fire-mist," or "nebulous mass" recognized by modern science, long ages are consumed and various definite stages are reached. The Secret Doctrine teaches that man, like the earth, existed potentially in the fire-mist, and that he has evolved downward into matter, *pari passu,* with the earth he inhabits, and of which he is an integral part.

Each human being is, therefore, a miniature earth (Microcosm) evolving within the greater earth (Macrocosm). This is one of the meanings of Ezekiel's "wheels within wheels." In a metaphysical sense, every so-called atom of matter is composed in the same way, and is going through a similar process. It may thus be seen that the key to the whole process of evolution is *Analogy.* It must naturally result from such a process, and from man's intimate relation to every principle, process, and plane that he epitomizes the whole; and that through expansion of consciousness, and differentiation throughout his long experience, when the consummation of evolution is reached, man will be at one with the All. Knowing and being will be One in him. Hence, he will be a god in the Platonic sense. This is precisely the view set forth by Herbert Spencer as the consummation of human evolution where absolute power and supreme knowledge result. Place over against this view of the infinite possibilities and transcendent destiny of man those of any of the exoteric religions or of materialistic science, and the old Wisdom Religion stands alone as the Divinest Revelation ever made to Humanity.

During the life of man in the animal body on the physical plane, he is composed of the seven principles. These are Atma, Buddhi, Manas, Kama, Astral Body, Life Principle, and Physical Body. (The order in which they are here named is from highest to lowest, or from spirit to matter.) The first three, namely, Atma, Buddhi, Manas, are symbolized by a triangle. This is the oldest "Trinity" known to man, and is the origin of all the "Trinities" in all the exoteric Religions of the World. As already shown, the Ineffable Name written in the Triangle refers to the One Universal Principle, antedating creation, and lying back of all evolution. *Christos* is called the *Word,* but is not Ain Soph. Atma in man represents Ain Soph in Cosmos. Hence it is called a "Spark of Divinity;" they are one in essence. Atma, Manas, and Buddhi represent Father, Son, and Holy Ghost. When Christ "ascended to the Father," he raised his consciousness to the seventh or Atmic Plane, and became in, fact (no longer in essence only) One With God.

These three principles in man compose the Spiritual Soul; the Immortal part of man; while Atma-Buddhi constitute the Higher-Self, the latent or potential God in man. The lower quaternary Body, Life-Principle, Form-Body and Kama (or Desire), are symbolized by a square. To make it plain, let us say that the triangle incarnates in the square: that is, the Soul (spiritual) "descends into matter." 'It has already been shown in a previous chapter what is the orderly relation of the seven principles. The Body is the *vehicle* of Life; Life is the *vehicle* of the Astral Body; the Astral Body is the *vehicle* of Kama; Kama is the *vehicle* of Manas; Manas is the *vehicle* of Buddhi; and Buddhi is the *vehicle* of Atma. This is the orderly relation or sequence of the principles. But as already shown, man is not a mere aggregation of principles, any more than he is a conglomerate aggregation of atoms, molecules, or cells. Just as atoms form molecules; molecules, cells; cells, tissues; tissues, organs; and organs, the whole body; so the Principles, while preserving a similar orderly sequence, in relation to each other, are, at the same time, *organized* in relation to the whole. That is, the Ego, the Thinker, unites with its *vehicle,* the Body.

Physiology has determined that certain functions are performed by certain organs, and that certain tracts are sensory, and others motor: that there are co-ordinating centers of motion, or of sensation, like the cerebellum, the medulla, or the sensory ganglia; and has assigned thought, memory, reason and volition, to the cerebrum. But neither physiology nor modern science has been able to arrive at the slightest conception as to what Mind, or Soul, really are, beyond functions of organs, or results of organization. Empirical facts in Hypnotism show processes actually taking place that can not be classified under any known physiological law.

The point at which the Triangle touches the square; that is, where the Spiritual-Soul forms its connecting link with the Physical-Body, is through Mind. *Kama* (the fourth principle, appetite, desire, passion, etc.) is not found in the upper triangle, but is the first in the square, or lower quaternary; and Kama has been called the *vehicle* of Manas. We have thus resulting from this association Kama-Manas; and the central organ of this conjoined or dual principle is the human brain. Here is the union of Thought and Sensation; or Knowing and Feeling; the union of the desire to know with the desire to feel. Here is, furthermore, the origin, seat, and nature of self-consciousness in man. On the upper side of the point of union we have the Will; on the lower side, Desire. This union of Manas with Kama, or Mind with Desire, is called the lower mind (Lower Manas), because it always involves the *personal equation*. Let the union exist, but the desire be entirely subordinate and impersonal, and the Higher-Mind becomes free. The terms of the personal equation are united with, or merged in the next higher. This is At-One-Ment of the lower man with the Divine: or Christ at-one with the Father. So long as the lower mind is held in bondage by desire, man can not seek or discern the Good or the True. He inquires, "What is good *for me?*" Freed from Desire, or the personal bias, he inquires after and seeks for that which is good or true *in itself.* When this condition is reached and habitually maintained, the square is said to be inclosed in the triangle. The whole lower nature is said to be at one with the Divine, or Spiritual Soul. Man's knowledge and power are no longer confined to, or circumscribed by, the lower plane, or the physical body; but, transcending these by Regeneration (self-conquest), and becoming perfect in Humanity, man attains Divinity. In other words, he becomes Christos. This is the meaning, aim, and consummation of Human Evolution; and this Philosophy defines the one-only process by which it may be attained. The Perfect Man is Christ: and Christ is God. This is the birthright and destiny of every human soul. It was taught in all the Greater Mysteries _of Antiquity, but the Exoteric creeds of Christendom, derived from the parables and allegories in which this doctrine was concealed from the ignorant and the profane, have accorded this Supreme Consummation to Jesus alone, and made it obscure or impossible for all the rest of humanity. In place of this, the grandest doctrine ever revealed to man, theologians have set up Salvation by Faith in a man-made Creed, and the Authority of the Church to "bind or lose on Earth or in Heaven." Law is annulled; Justice, dethroned; Merit, ignored; Effort, discouraged; and Sectarianism, Atheism, and Materialism are the results.

All real Initiation is an internal, not an external, process. The outer ceremony is dead and useless only so far as it symbolizes and illustrates, and thereby makes clear the inward change. The ceremony instructs, but it cannot transform. To transform means to regenerate; and this comes by trial, by effort, by self-conquest, by sorrow, disappointment, *failure;* and a daily renewal of the conflict. It is thus that man must "work out his own salvation." The consummation of initiation is the Perfect Master, the Christos, for these are the same. They "are the goal, the perfect consummation of human evolution.

Now, with this idea of human evolution, and in the light of modern science, what is it to be a Master? Not a mythical Master, not one so holy, so Divine, so incomprehensible as to be the object of blind worship alone, and impossible to be imitated, an Idol, a Fetish, but one indeed to reverence, to love, and, above all, to approach and imitate; an Elder Brother, a Compassionate Teacher, a Helper of the Human Race.

By constant struggle and daily conflict the Master has conquered self. Life after life he has gathered experience. Truly hath he been a "man of sorrows and acquainted with grief." He has assailed all problems; studied all sciences; exhausted all litanies; apprehended all philosophies; practiced all arts. At every step he has loved and helped humanity more and more, and sought his own desires less and less. Grown familiar thus with all the lower planes of life by sore trial, by bitter conflict, by frequent defeat, by hope deferred, almost despairing, he has at last renounced self utterly, and so become "dead to the world." This is the "Great Renunciation." An Infinite Compassion for all that lives takes possession of his soul, and an infinite peace settles within his spirit.

"Believe thou not that sitting in dark forests, in proud seclusion and apart from man; believe thou not that life on roots and plants, that thirst assuaged with snow from the great Range; believe thou not, O Devotee, that this will lead thee to the goal of final liberation."

"Step out from sunlight into shade, to make more room for others." ...

"'Tis from the bud of Renunciation of the Self that springs the sweet fruit of final liberation."

"The selfish devotee lives to no purpose. The man who does not go through his appointed work in life has lived in vain."

"So shalt thou be in full accord with all that lives; bear love to men as though they were thy brother-pupils, disciples of one Teacher, the sons of one sweet mother."

"Compassion speaks and saith: Can there be bliss when all that lives must suffer? Shalt thou be saved and hear the whole world cry?" [1]

But, says some modern Agnostic, this is all beautiful, very fine indeed, but mere sentiment; with no foundation in fact, and no possible realization in the life of man. It will do for sentimental women, for tramps, or lunatics. What, then, is the meaning, and what the goal of human evolution? Is Tantalus the one Divinity of the universe?

Turning now from the ethical side of the problem to the scientific, let us see what happens as the consciousness of man remounts from the lower animal-self toward the spiritual soul; from the physical toward the higher planes.

We have shown Mind (Manas) to be the connecting link between the "Upper Triad" and the "Lower Quaternary." When man has once passed the plane of Savagery in his evolution, Mind becomes more and more apparent as the battle-ground of his evolution. He gradually relaxes tooth and claw, and, first, by instinct, then by cunning, and finally by reason and design, pursues the struggle for existence. He changes continually his code of ethics, for he is continually compelled to compromise, and he finds that he can retain more by relinquishing a part. His very selfishness leads him to combine and co-operate with his fellows. At last his sympathies expand. By and by he learns that a "fellow feeling makes us wondrous kind." He reciprocates, and at last becomes generous. During all this long and weary struggle his mind is enlarging, and his consciousness expanding. He creates for himself a world of Thought. It is unreal and unsatisfying, because so impermanent; and yet he struggles on. He reflects over his varied experience; seeks causes, and discerns principles. He realizes the saying, "My mind to me a kingdom is;" "On Earth there is nothing great but Man: In Man there is nothing great but Mind." Or, the older saying, "All that I am is the result of what I have Thought." Mind is like an alembic in which are precipitated all experiences.

By evolution man is continually climbing upward to higher planes. His five senses are adjusted to observations and experiences of the physical plane; but he has other experiences. The senses are narrow and circumscribed; yet even these become refined. His tastes alter, his tendencies ascend. He is reaching outward as his sympathies expand, and upward, as his ideals become higher. There is revealed to him a whole world of experience in which the lower senses play no part: A world of aspiration in which Self is not the goal. The very physical bounds of self are loosening, expanding, disappearing. Hitherto he has been conscious of flashes of intuition; of knowing things he has seemingly never learned. He sees inner meanings, and senses subtler powers. Not only in visions and intuitions of the day, but in dreams of the night he has experiences beyond the bounds of sense. He learns the power of Thought. By conquering Self, his Will becomes strong. By subduing passion, his mind becomes clear. He has premonitions of coming events; for all events and thoughts and things exist first on higher planes, and are precipitated thence into matter. He becomes clairaudient and clairvoyant. He has broken the bonds of Self and now functions on higher planes. As his senses and organs on the physical plane made him Master there of brutes, and of physical nature, even so on the higher plane, the senses and organs evolved by the same Evolutionary Law of experience and choice, make him, on the higher plane, Master of men and of higher Nature. All the time he is evolving organs and functions, and dealing with matter and force. Just as experience and reflection taught him the laws and processes of the physical plane, so his expanded and refined experience and intuitions (spiritual perceptions) teach him the laws of the higher plane.

But, says the physiologist, on the physical plane man has evolved physical organs which bring him in contact with Nature on that plane. Even so it is on all planes, for analogy is the key of interpretation, "As below, so above."

Deep within the recesses of the skull, lying at the base of the brain, is a curious little structure known as the Pineal Gland — with the Restiform bodies. Modern physiology assigns to it no function. Des Cartes called it "the seat of the soul." In the average individual it is small and apparently useless, though its focalized position and symmetrical relations to surrounding structures would seem to assign to it some very important office. It presents a different appearance in the very young, the very old, and in the idiotic, from that found in the prime of life, health, and vigor. It has been called "The Third Eye." The Ancient Hindoos called it the Eye of Siva, and it should be borne in mind that Siva is the third person in the Hindoo Trinity, and is the Renewer, or Regenerator (not simply the Destroyer). The action of this little "gland" may be likened to the bridge of a violin. It renders the nerve chords more tense, and thus *raises the vibrations* of the brain tissues. It is atrophied, and therefore dormant in the average individual, because the relaxed chords (using a symbol) correspond to the vibrations on the physical plane; and it is one of the well-known laws of physiology that every organ will become atrophied from disuse.

Going back to our problem of Consciousness, we find Mind to be the changes in our states of consciousness: orderly, when governed by the Will, and guided by Reason; disorderly, when swayed by the passions, or led by caprice. All the so-called Senses are differentiations of the One-Sense-Consciousness (Apperception).

Reference has elsewhere been made to empirical proof that in the case of Sight and Hearing; or, Light, Color, and Sound, the vibrations are consonant and interchangeable. Now it can easily be seen that if the one sense (consciousness) has differentiated into several Senses, so-called, in man's "descent" from higher to lower planes, on his "ascent" from lower to higher planes, the differentiations must gradually disappear, and one center may combine and synthesize two or more Senses. This is precisely what happens in the case of hearing and seeing, or in the vibrations producing sound and color. Since empirical science has demonstrated the fact, the theory may now, perhaps, no longer excite only a sneer; for it must be borne in mind that the foregoing is one of the theories taught in the Ancient Mysteries.

Here then is the physiological, no less than the philosophical basis of Clairvoyance and Clairaudience.

The Eye of Siva is, in fact, an All-Seeing-Eye; for it practically annuls Space and Time as concepts on the physical plane.

Whether or not modern Masonry has any such tradition, or any such metaphysical or scientific concept regarding the All-Seeing-Eye so conspicuous in its symbolism, such, at least, is its meaning in the Secret Doctrine of Antiquity.

A real Master, then, has the Eye of Siva; the pineal gland, dormant in others, is active in him; and the vibrations of his brain correspond to the synthesis of sound and light. Henceforth, for him, Space and Time are no longer illusions, as he lives in the one and is Master of all lower planes. Says the Voice of the Silence —

"Alas, alas, that men should possess Alaya, be one with the great Soul, and that possessing it, Alaya should so little avail."

"Unless thou hearest thou canst not see."
"Unless thou seest thou canst not hear."
"To hear and see, this is the second stage."

So much as to the meaning of the word Master, and the methods by which Adeptship is attained.

Now, as to the nature of the Power he possesses, or, the Master's Word. A man's words express his ideas, and reveal his character. In this sense the creative power of Deity is called the Word of God, or the Logos; and the whole process of creation, being an outward expression of Divinity, is called the Logos.

"There is in Nature one most potent force, by means whereof a single man, who could possess himself of it, and should know how to direct it, could revolutionize and change the face of the world.

"This force was known to the ancients. It is a universal agent, whose Supreme Law is equilibrium, and whereby, if science can but learn how to control it, it will be possible to change the order of the Seasons; to produce in night the phenomena of day; to send a thought in an instant around the world; to heal or slay at a distance; to give our words universal success, and make them reverberate everywhere."

"This agent, partially revealed by the blind guesses of the disciples of Mesmer, is precisely what the Adepts of the middle ages called the 'elementary matter of the Great Work.' The Gnostics held that it composed the igneous body of the Holy Spirit; and it was adored in the secret rites of the Sabbat or the Temple, under the hieroglyphic figure of Baphomet, or the hermaphroditic goat of Mendes." [2]

Modern Science is slowly re-discovering *some* of the secrets of Antiquity. The "Radiant matter" of Professor Crooks, the Cathode ray of Roentgen, and other advancements in psychic photography, the *Mayava Rupa* of Baraduc, and, greatest of all, the discoveries of J. W. Keely, trench so closely on the "elementary matter" of the old Alchemists and the *Akas* of the more ancient Adepts of old India, that a student of occultism need no longer be afraid to reveal himself.

There is an old legend which declares that the ancient Atlanteans, not those of Plato's island which was a fragment of the great continent, but of the Continent which sank, it is said, 50,000 years ago, possessed the secret of this "most potent force," referred to by Bro. Pike, that they were great Magicians, and that they did thus "change the face of the earth," as Bro. Pike declares possible, and that the sinking of the continent was the result. Perhaps, if our "rain-makers" succeed in solving a little further the problem of *vibrations* in their relations to atmospheric changes, this and many other ancient "Fables" may seem less fabulous to modern "scientific materialism." When it is stated that these terrible forces exist, and may be known and utilized, people are not scandalized in this age of dynamite. But when it is also stated that the knowledge of these forces is concealed from all but trained Adepts who have demonstrated their unqualified beneficence to man, and that in the hands of vicious, unqualified, or ignorant persons, they are capable of working untold misery to man, the statement usually excites derision.

If this embargo were removed, doubtless mankind would not long remain in any uncertainty as to the existence of the terrible will of Bulwer Lytton. If it were revealed to the Spanish Generals or the Cuban Rebels at the present time, the contest would soon be ended on that unhappy island.

This force is the universal Life agent, as Bro. Pike says, "wherein are two natures and a double current of love and wrath." This ambient fluid penetrates everything. Hence it is the "First Matter" of the Alchemists. It is concentrated in man as the magnetic living force directed by the Will. He who knows its "chord of mass" or the "key-note" of its vibrations can, by his Will, waken it from Space and send it in mighty waves to do his bidding. The real *Word* of the Master, therefore, in a scientific sense, is this *tone-key* by which the "Principalities and Powers of the Air" can be made to do his bidding. That any one should possess such power and withhold its use, is not easily conceived by the average man of today; and that such a Master should also conceal his own existence, seems altogether incredible to an age of Syndicates, and Trades Unionists. Such a power would, indeed, be a knockdown argument in all competition, and furnish a very ready way of settling all disputes.

The ethical training to which reference has been made, and which began at the first step of initiation, preceded all scientific training in the ancient mysteries; and the Masters are spoken of by Plato, Iamblichus, and many other writers, as the "Immortal Gods." But it must not be concluded that because the real Master does not enter into competition on the physical plane, or parade his gifts for the applause of men, that he makes no use of his sublime Wisdom and transcendent Powers. It would be childish to use such powers for display, to awe the ignorant, or to amuse the curious; and such Men have long since put away childish things. From their secure retreat on the inner or higher planes of being, they influence, but do not dominate the affairs of men; and many a beneficent movement is due to their timely aid.

According to our conception of energy as correlative throughout Nature's boundless domain, Fohat is the synthesis of all the so-called forces of nature. It is "Cosmic Electricity Endowed with Intelligence." In the manifested Universe, Fohat is "that Occult electric vital power, which, under the Will of the Creative Logos, unites and brings together all forms, giving them the first impulse which becomes in time law." It is "the Constructive Force of Cosmic Electricity." Fohat has "seven sons, who are also his brothers." [3] These are Electricity, Magnetism, Sound, Light, Heat, Cohesion, etc. What modern science calls the "modes of motion," can fairly be called definite vibrations. The forces just named all manifest on the lower physical plane. That is, we see there their effects. If back of all forces there is One Force, and if this one force differentiates first into seven, and these seven are in their turn divisible into other Sevens, we get the idea that the Solar spectrum and the musical scale reveal the universal modulus; and that what is known to exist in the realm of Light and Sound, must also exist in the realm of Electricity, Chemism; and, in short, with every force and on every plane in Nature. [4] If, therefore, one can discover the rate of vibration, the quality and amplitude of the "wave-length" in any given case, he will hold the *Key* to that plane.

Fohat is not only the synthesis of all known forces, and endowed with intelligence, but *potentially,* before differentiation begins, is the Author of the Law of all subsequent correlations, differentiations, or action whatsoever.

If this view is considered carelessly it might seem to involve materialism or pantheism. But such is not the case. When one realizes that Fohat is one of the highest of the Elohim, or Builders, the Creators spoken of in Genesis, the direct agents of Divinity through which the *Ancient of Days* or *Ain Soph* creates, this view will be seen to be spiritual to the last degree.

The first impulse of Fohat becomes, in time, the law of all subsequent vibration. Fohat is, moreover, in the Secret Doctrine, likened to an "Intelligent Force moved by Will."

As the various forces and planes in the constitution of man are derived from and correspond to similar forces and planes in Nature, it can readily be seen what potencies are latent in man; and that the possession of the knowledge of these planes and forces, and a Trained Will to use and direct them, would naturally constitute one an Adept, or Master. The mere power of thought or of the imagination, with a strong concentration of will power, would, at all times, enable a real Master to say, "take notice thereof, and let it be done." The ignorant would naturally say: "What manner of man is this, that even the winds and the waves obey him?"

It is said of the Word A. U. M. that it has seven meanings applicable to seven planes, requiring, therefore, seven keys; and similar traditions exist with regard to the Tetragramaton of the Kabalah — "He who maketh the earth to quake and angels and men to tremble" — even Jehovah. For the ignorant and superstitious, this has one meaning. For the intelligent student of Kabalah, it has many and very different meanings.

The physical plane, that of the body of man, is such by virtue of the co-ordinate vibrations of all the principles that enter into its construction. The physical exists by virtue of the maintenance of the Key or *dominant chord* of that plane. As long as this key can be maintained in perfect concord, health exists. Whenever the harmony is disturbed, disease results; and when the key can no longer exist, dissolution of the organism occurs, and death is the result.

The problem of genuine initiation, or training in occultism, consists in placing all the operations of the body under the dominion of the will; in freeing the Ego from the dominion of the appetites, passions, and the whole lower nature. The idea is not to despise the body, but to purify it; not to destroy the appetites, but to elevate and control them absolutely. This mastery of the lower nature does not change the Key of the physical nature as such; but subordinates it to that of a higher plane. Without this subordination, the clamorous lower animal nature drowns out all higher vibrations; as if in an orchestra the bass-viols and the drums only could be heard; and noise, rather than harmony, would result. Hence the old saying — "He that conquers himself is greater than he who taketh a city."

From such mastery of the lower nature by intelligent effort and Will power, there results not only peace, the silencing of the clamorous lower nature, but clearness of vision and power of discernment. There results also a sense of freedom and of power, and a certainty of Knowledge. In the Bhagavad Gita this training is called Yoga, and is denned as *equal-mindedness* and *skill in the performance of actions.* It is distinguished from Hatha Yoga, which is mere straining after special powers (mediumship), and is called Raja Yoga; that of the Kingly or Divine sort; and is everywhere portrayed as a permanent subjugation of the whole lower nature. It is, in fact, in science and in a philosophical sense, the higher evolution of man. Whatever is gained in one life in this direction is carried over to the next incarnation; while all apparent gain of "powers" in Hatha Yoga (mediumship) is lost in future births, or else is a detriment to evolution.

The potency of the planes in man increases from the lower to the higher, and the whole process we have been considering consists symbolically, in "placing the square within the triangle:" that is, of so purifying the whole lower nature as to make it at-one with the higher. The mind that functions through the physical brain, governed by the senses and appetites, and that first gives man self-consciousness, now moves one plane higher. Passion no longer rules the man and blinds him to universal laws and higher principles. The Higher Self in man, called his "God," or *Christos,* was formerly "crucified between two thieves;" namely, the Higher and Lower Manas. Hence the saying, "when I would do good, evil is present with me." As the body is crucified (a symbol of death and suffering), the Christos says to one of the thieves — "This day shalt thou be with me in paradise." This refers to the Higher Manas, now freed from the lower nature. The other "thief," or the brain mind, is left to perish with the physical body of Christos on the Cross of Time. It may thus be seen how the battle-ground of man's lower nature with the higher is the mind, and that self-conquest and the higher evolution are synonymous. The process of this evolution can be expressed in mathematics and terms of exact science. Hence the old saying in the Bible — "I praise thee with my lips, *I know not the numbers.*" Silence the dominant chord of the lower animal nature, and change the vibration to that of the Higher Mind, and "Thou shalt become as gods knowing good and evil."

This change of vibration, with a knowledge of the dominant chord and the combination of the keyboard directed by the Will, is the discovery of J. W. Keely. The Roentgen ray is one of the "seven forces" into which light, sqund and electricity are divisible. The secret of the Crooks tubes has been clearly shown to consist in getting rid of a surplus of molecules or atoms, and thereby increasing the vibration (bombardment) of the remainder; and thus liberating, not creating, a "new light." The trained will of the Adept can do this, and more. He has been seen to make his whole body luminous. Since the experiments of Von Reichenbach have been verified, and the "illusion-body" photographed, such a result can no longer be declared to be a scientific impossibility.

It should be borne in mind that our entire philosophy as related to man proceeds from the empirical *fact* of Consciousness, with appeal taken at every step to the facts of experience. Our theory does not consist in any speculation or assertion regarding the nature of consciousness itself, but rather in using both facts and experiences in the natural order of their relations. In the case of the Master or Adept, the same potencies and processes are involved as in ordinary evolution; and none others. The different results arise from the fact that in the case of the Adept, these ordinary processes are no longer trammeled or delayed.

"The *Wise Ones* tarry not in pleasure-grounds of the senses."

'The *Wise Ones* heed not the sweet-tongued voices of illusions."

"Thou shalt not let thy senses make a play-ground of thy mind." [5]

It may thus be seen that neither causes nor results are involved in an untried "working hypothesis."

This philosophy not only explains the nature and origin of all the Christs of history, as the result of evolution under natural law, but these all stand as "Landmarks," pointing out "the Way, the Life and the Truth," in the journey of the soul, and the immortal destiny of man. Furthermore, every point herein made is but a crude fragment derived from the Ancient Mysteries, held by the Gnostics and early Christians, and embodied in or implied by the parables, allegories, and glyphs of Freemasonry.

Initiation therefore must be seen to be both evolutionary and regenerative; and not a mere empty farce or a dead ceremony.

Taking now this evolutionary process as a fact, we may profitably consider further the change that occurs in the structure of man's complex organism as evolution proceeds.

We have shown Mind to be the active theater in which the real battle is fought for the supremacy of the Higher or Spiritual-Soul, as distinguished from the lower Animal-Soul.

"Thou shalt not let thy senses make a play-ground of the mind." No doubt many who have read this sentence have regarded it as a moral precept only ignorant, perhaps, of the fact that there is not only a philosophical concept but scientific facts and Laws back of all moral truths.

The mind is the realm of thought, and the sum of all experience on both the physical (senses and feelings) and metaphysical (reason, imagination, Will, intuition, etc.) sides of Consciousness. Experience may be called the moving panorama of events in the conscious life of man. Thought is, therefore, the changes in our states of consciousness. Thought is the active movement, and consciousness the passive theater of the varied experiences of life. Consciousness is, therefore, to the life of man what Space is to the existence and movements of Cosmos — the **all-container**. The Ego is a self-centered "ray;" a focus; the "mathematical point" in consciousness. That which the nucleus is to the living cell, the point from which all forces and movements emanate, and to which all counter-movements and forces tend, such is the Ego — the Thinker of man. The first point to be made in real initiation is for the Thinker to control the thought. Instead of passively and helplessly receiving all suggestions that come from the physical senses, or appetites; or all that come from ambition, selfishness and pride; he selects, and chooses, and Wills what thoughts shall come. In this manner he acquires mastery over his own mind, and frees his will from the dominion of Desire; or rather elevates and purifies Desire. He is no longer hag-ridden by vagrant thoughts; or a victim to the ghosts of a remorseful memory, or a depraved imagination. That one can thus choose the subjects of his own thoughts is really within the experience of every one when he comes to reflect upon the subject. But few people are aware that the mind can be divested of all thought on the physical or brain-side of experience. Yet what is revery, or day-dream, or absent-mindedness? We have only to analyze and reflect on our ordinary experiences in order to see how natural and really commonplace are the operations of these occult laws.

When this process is intelligently conceived and persisted in, the mind grows clear and the Will strong, and for this change there is a physical basis and a scientific law; and there must be corresponding changes in the physical structure. This change occurs on the Kamic plane, Which is now subordinated to Reason and Will; and also in the Astral or Form-body, which is the vehicle of Kama (passion and desire). This Astral body is the mold or pattern around which the physical structure is built, which it precedes and survives for a short time after death. In relation to the molecules and cells which constitute the tissues of the body the Astral structure is Atomic. The Astral body of each separate incarnation is the immediate result of the thoughts and experiences of the preceding life; modified, however, by all previous lives. It is invisible to ordinary vision, but, fortified by the strong dregs of Karma, in a gross and passionate individual, it may appear as the Ghost of Wraith seen at times near cemeteries. It has also much to do with the "ghosts" and "materializations" of the Seance rooms. This Astral principle, like all the other seven (really six, exclusive of the highest) is sevenfold in its constitution in man; and it is the lowest of which we have been speaking. This Astral is one of the principles of the "square," or lower quaternary, and is not, therefore, the real spiritual soul, or immortal part in man.

With this crude outline of the Form-Body we may now return to the process of regeneration. The change resulting from self-mastery and the subjugation of the lower animal nature, strengthens the Form-Body and liberates it from the physical shell. Instead of this Astral or Form-Body saturated with the gross animal spirits (kama) being held to the vibrations of the mere animal and physical nature, and thus holding consciousness to the key-note of the physical plane, involved in the lower animal life, the vibrations are now raised one plane higher. The action of the Pineal Gland and Restiform Bodies heretofore described, now come into play with the purified and liberated Form-Body. The physical body is still the vehicle of the Ego *on the physical plane;* but it is no longer a dark prison-house with animal lust and pride as Goalers. It is a common experience, and often consciously so, that we "journey when we sleep." We go out of the body and visit scenes, and gain experiences during the sleep of the physical senses, but it is rare that we remember, or really understand what happens, for the reason that all that we know as memory concerns the brain on the lower side. Now, in case of the growing Adept these experiences become continually more frequent and lucid. He retains distinct recollection, and understands more and more of what occurs. By and by he observes the process of "going out" and "coming back;" and at length learns to repeat the process at will; a perfectly natural evolution, be it observed. The story of Peter Ibbetson gives an exceedingly graphic and philosophical description of this "double consciousness," which is more than justified by the phenomena of Hypnotism and Somnambulism. The Adept from the time he is able to change at will his habitat, leads a double life, and lives at once in two worlds. He has, moreover, "put the last enemy under foot." He has, by self-conquest and Will, conquered Death. These are they whom Plato and the old Initiates call the Immortals. At the death or dissolution of the physical body such a one is not precipitated into a new world, as a helpless infant is born into the physical, with organs undeveloped, and functions untried; but, already familiar with the inner realm from experience, he preserves consciousness on that plane and is there like an adult on the physical plane. It is true that he can not function or manifest on the physical plane as before, for he has now no longer the physical body. But he has learned to live so little on that plane, and found thereon so little of real enjoyment, that unless he has a special work to do for humanity, or an obligation to discharge to others, he finds nothing to regret in dying. He has fulfilled the Law of Necessity (Karma) by *obeying* it!

'This is peace,
To conquer love of self and lust of life,
To tear deep-rooted passion from the breast,
To still the inward strife."

"For love, to clasp Eternal Beauty close;
For glory, to be Lord of self, for pleasure
To live beyond the gods; for countless wealth
To lay up lasting treasure."

"Then sorrow ends, for Life and Death have ceased:
How should lamps flicker when their oil is spent?
The old sad count is clear, the new is clean;
Thus hath a man content."

"Hark! from the deep unfathomable vortex of that golden light in which the Victor bathes *All Nature's* wordless voice in thousand tones ariseth to proclaim: "*Joy unto ye, oh men of Myalba.*

"*A Pilgrim Hath Returned back from the other shore.*"

"*A new Arhan is born*" [6]

Such in philosophy, in science, in fact, and in truth is a Master; as the natural product of self-conquest and evolution, and not as a miraculous creation.

The knowledge possessed by such a Master, and the power which he finds subject to his Will, are derived, as in all ordinary cases, from the whole range of his experience. One has only to use good judgment and thoughtful observation in experimenting along the lines indicated, and to go but a little way to become convinced of the truth involved in the philosophy of self-conquest. It is no "go-as-you-please"' evolution. It is rather using the Will and subordinating the lower nature to accomplish "the Will of God concerning us;" in place of ringing the everlasting changes in sensation and ennui life after life upon earth. In comparison with the ordinary process of drifting with any tide, it is, indeed, a forcing process; but the force is derived from the higher nature, and the result is plainly within the law of man's moral and intellectual life.

The term Astral-Body has been used because it is somewhat familiar to Western students. The term is a very loose one at best, and the plane and structure to which it refers are so metaphysical and complex that it is difficult to find terms in which to describe it. The conception of what we ordinarily call "matter and force" is, moreover, entirely inadequate in dealing with such problems. Electricity, for example, is not simply a "mode of motion," or a "fluid," but a correlate involving life and intelligence, with latent consciousness, and moved by Will: a duality in itself, according as it manifests as the substance of one plane or the energy of another.

Furthermore, the problem of consciousness as related to Space and Time already pointed out, makes it difficult to put in exact terms the experience of the Ego on the supra-physical planes. In "going out of the body," for example, there is a freeing of the centers of action always resident in the Astral, or the Atomic Body, from the physical organs and tissues; and a consequent change of the planes of consciousness. Synchronous vibrations now occur between the centers of consciousness in the Astral-Body and the whole Astral Plane; just as before, this synchronism existed between the physical body and the physical plane in relation to physical consciousness. The Astral-Body, therefore, need not leave the vicinity of the physical, or "travel through space," to take cognizance of events elsewhere transpiring. This, furthermore, remains true, even in cases where the apparition of the individual is seen at great distances from where the physical body is, at the time, reposing. [7] Thought is, in every case, a vibration molding substance into definite forms. Whenever we think of a person near or far, we create a thought image of that person. This form necessarily varies according to the clearness of memory or imagination, and the strength of Will. Furthermore, our thought is characteristic of ourselves, and in thinking intently of a distant object or person, a thought-form of ourselves may appear at that place. This may occur or be visible to others, and exist unconsciously to ourselves. With a person of trained habits of thought, who thinks clearly and connectedly, and who is possessed of a strong will; who knows, also, how to fix and hold the thought on an object or a person, the projection of the Thought-Body, as above described, becomes a comparatively easy matter. Such an Illusion might or might not be perceived by another; nor, except in the case of an Adept, could the individual causing the Illusion be certain himself whether his experiment had been successful or not.

While these facts have been familiar to students of occultism for ages, they have seldom been discussed in print for the reason that such discussion could do no good and would only excite ridicule. But now that modern scientific experiment trenches so closely on the subject, the discussion may not seem so unprofitable.

In a communication from Paris dated June 27, 1896, a description of psychic photography is given as presented to the Paris Academie de Medicine by Dr. Baraduc:

"Dr. Baraduc explains in part his methods of psychic photography, which seem simple enough. The experimenter locks himself in a dark room where he has previously placed a sensitive plate. After seating himself and divesting his mind of vagrant thoughts and deliberations, and after steadying his nerves, he concentrates ail his ideas on a certain image, be it man, beast, or inanimate object, and it will be found that the accuracy of the image will be in proportion to the power of his will. If no other image has intruded, a perfect likeness will have been obtained. In conclusion, Dr. Baraduc says that not everybody has this power to control his volition, and in order to succeed, a strong imagination is absolutely necessary, and an energetic Will indispensable."

Mr. James M. Rusk, of Ohio, reports the same result from a similar experiment made by himself and confirmed by Colonel De Rochas.

The only new feature in these experiments is the introduction of photography and the consequent fixation of the images, and this result is, of course, of paramount importance to materialistic science. Ten thousand persons will be convinced by a fact or an ocular demonstration, where one will perceive the truth from reason, philosophy, or intuition. Let us have the ocular demonstration, then, by all means. Experiment might be facilitated immensely by assistance derived from the old philosophy, but as this is usually ignored or derided, Science will have a long and toilsome journey before it apprehends the real nature of these illusory images, or deduces from experiment the nature of the Soul. The death-knell of materialism is, however, already sounded. "For this, and that which we are about to receive, the Lord make us truly thankful!"

[1] Voice of the Silence.
[2] Morals and Dogma, p. 734.
[3] See Plate I.
[4] See Plate I.
[5] Voice of the Silence.
[6] Voice of the Silence.
[7] Dr. Baraduc has demonstrated this, by the "Thought-Body."

Chapter Seven - The Secret Doctrine (Continued)

The Sign of the Master.

It must not be supposed that in the Ancient Mysteries every Initiate became a Master in the sense outlined in the preceding chapters. There were the Lesser and the Greater Mysteries. To the Lesser all were eligible; to the Greater, very few; and of these few, fewer still were ever exalted to the sublime and last degree. Some remained for a lifetime in the lower degrees, unable to progress further on account of constitutional defect or mental and spiritual incapacity. The Mysteries unfolded the Building of Worlds, the Religion of Nature, the Brotherhood of Man, the Immortality of the Soul, and the Evolution of Humanity. No ceremony was artificial and meaningless; no symbol, however grotesque to the ignorant, was merely fanciful.

"It is not in the books of the Philosophers, but in the religious symbolism of the Ancients, that we must look for the footprints of Science, and rediscover the Mysteries of Knowledge. The Priests of Egypt knew better than we do the laws of movement and of life..." [1]

Philosophy, however, may give us a Key to symbolism, a Universal Modulus. True philosophy discerns the Plans drawn by Divinity on the Tracing Board of Time for the building of Cosmos.

The Primary Concepts of such a Philosophy are few and simple. So, indeed, are the root-forms in Symbolism. The changes rung on concept and Symbol, as the plan unfolds, become more and more complex, even where they are wrought *by those who know*. When from these the symbolism descends to parable and allegory in order to clothe the primary concept in ethical language, and make it apprehensible and binding to the ignorant masses, its garment and Fiat read, "Thus saith the Lord."

When, however, Ignorance in high places, or cupidity and lust for power interpret, or willfully suppress, disfigure and distort the ancient symbols, as has been done for lo, these many centuries, the masses are not prepared to believe that the real truth, uncontaminated by man, has ever been discovered. The vandals have done their work better and more successfully in thus blotting out all belief in the existence of the Old Wisdom, than in destroying the records of the Truth itself. The real symbols are the Modulus of Nature, and man can never destroy these.

"Thales and Pythagoras learned in the Sanctuaries of Egypt that the Earth revolved around the Sun, but they did not attempt to make this generally known, because to do so it would have been necessary to reveal one of the great Secrets of the Temple, the double law or attraction and radiation, or of sympathy and antipathy, of fixedness and movement, which is the principle of creation and the perpetual cause of life. This truth was ridiculed by Lactanius, as it was long after sought to be proven a falsehood by persecution by Papal Rome."

"So the Philosophers reasoned, while the Priests, without replying to them or even smiling at their errors, wrote in those Hieroglyphics that created all dogmas and all poetry, the Secrets of Truth." [2]

To preserve its authority and its perquisites, Ecclesiasticism will, today, as in all the past, answer such statements with neither facts, reason, nor arguments, but *with a curse!!* and so long as men grovel with fear at the curse will the truth be concealed. When men are wise enough and brave enough to defy both the anathema and the anathematizer, the whole opposition to light and progress will fall to pieces. Till then, the ignorant masses, imitating their superiors, will scout, ridicule and slander all who speak the truth. Freedom and Enlightenment are the only real Saviors of Mankind; while Ignorance is the father of Superstition, and Selfishness the parent of Vice.

The Ideal in Church and State, the *motive* for the Ecclesiastical and Political Hierarchies, has been in all ages to govern men professedly for their own good. The Secret Doctrine teaches man to govern himself. So long as Hierarchies subordinate all things to the real benefit of man, and give Light and Knowledge to all in such measure as they are capable of receiving, they are a blessing and not a curse. When, however, the Potentate suppresses Knowledge, claims power by Divine Right, or by inheritance, rather than by proof of knowledge and by service done to man; when ignorance or disbelief is punished as a crime and men torture the body, or agonize the mind under that devil's plea — "to save the Soul" — then does the Hierarchy become an enemy of both God and Man.

Neither Political nor Religious Hierarchy has ever existed for any great length of time in the outer world without becoming corrupt. The continuance of power in such cases must always depend on the ignorance of the people; therefore, the Hierarchy will resist to the utmost the spread of true enlightenment. It is for this reason that for many centuries the Secret Doctrine and all of its students or expounders have been under ban of the Church, and of the State, whenever Ecclesiasticism has been able to form an alliance therewith. Persecution in every form, for opinions' sake, is ever the sign-manual of worldliness and irreligion. It is the rule of Might against Right, and the trampling under foot of the weak and helpless by the strong and powerful; and to complete the blasphemy, and monument the cruelty, such persecution is generally enacted "in the name of the Lord."

The Altars of Masonry have ever been the Beacon-Lights of Liberty; and the Lodge a City of Refuge; a Sanctuary of Knowledge and Protection to the way-faring Brother of all Nations and tongues. Patterning after the Sanctuaries of the Ancient Mysteries, and founded on the principle of the Universal and Unqualified Brotherhood of Man, they have held aloft the Torch of Liberty. If in later times class distinctions and color lines have divided the craft, the Lodge has never resorted to persecution, or been the agent of oppression. When these veils that have for the time obscured the true light are re-moved, and every man is regarded for his intrinsic worth alone, and Masonry is indeed and in truth no respecter of persons, then will this great organiza-tion enter on an era of prosperity such as is its heritage from all the past, and its right by the simple power of *Brotherly Love, Relief* and *Truth*.

The traditions of Masonry in later times exclude woman from participating in the work of the Lodge, but not from all the rights and benefits of the Craft. The reasons that have led to the exclusion of women need not here be dis-cussed. A sufficient answer to all advocates of Androgynous Masonry may be found in the history of all attempts to establish or to revive it. Each and all have failed, and have generally proved fruitful of discord and scandal. Nor is woman either the loser or the most to blame for this result. The Ancient Mys-teries were organized schools of learning, and knowledge was the signal of progress and the basis of Fellowship. In modern Masonry Fraternity alone has usurped the place of Wisdom, and in the service of the Lodge to mankind its great work has been to preserve unaltered the Ancient Landmarks as a heritage to posterity. Every true Mason for centuries has thus been a Soldier of the Truth, fighting for its Altars and its Fires. In this work of the Lodge woman could have been of no service.

While every true Mason is the most loyal of men to every office of woman, as Mother, Sister, Daughter and Wife; as Companion, Friend, and Inspirer of man, he would have been trammeled by her presence in the Lodge, and she would have received no benefit by being admitted. When, however, the days of Ritualism alone are ended, when from the one duty of guarding the altars and lighting the camp-fires, Masonry resumes its prerogative as Teacher and Enlightener of mankind, and the Philosophy of Nature and of Life are unfold-ed in its Schools and Colleges as with the Maji of old, and when with no fear of persecution from timeserving Potentate or Creed-ridden Priest, the Light may shine for all, then will the doors of real initiation be as open to woman as to man, as was the case in the schools of Pythagoras as shown by Iamblichus. The Ancient Wisdom concerned itself largely with the Souls of men, and undertook to elevate the earthly life by purifying the Soul and ex-alting its Ideals. It teaches that souls are sexless; and that the sex of the body is an incident of gestation. No civilization known to man has ever risen to any great heights, or long maintained its supremacy, that debased woman. In-deed, the Secret Doctrine demonstrates with unmistakable clearness that sexual debasement in any form is the highway to degeneracy and destruction of both man and woman; and of Nations quite as certainly as of individuals.

The most debased and horrible chapters in human history are recorded in scientific works by medical experts. Atavism is here exemplified as nowhere else. Here, more than anywhere else within the possible experience of man, lies the "Sin against the Holy Ghost;" for through this open door, through which rush the most unholy passions and the hellish fires of lust, it is possi-ble for man to *lose his human soul* and descend to the animals. If any one doubts this, let him read — if he can — some of the scientific medical works on Sex-perverts, and then consult the attendant physicians of the insane and the symptoms and records of Lunacy.

'The first lesson we are taught in Masonry is to be good men and true." And the first declaration made by the neophyte in Masonry is that he comes to the Lodge to "learn to subdue his passions, and improve himself in Masonry," i.e., to engage in the building of a fit temple for an indwelling soul.

It may thus be seen that all the traditions and usages of Masonry agree fully with the philosophy of the Secret Doctrine as to true Initiation, and that both are justified by all experience, by all history, and by all scientific discovery and advancement up to date. These ancient institutions, derided, anathematized, misrepresented, persecuted, and *suppressed,* as they have been for the last fifteen hundred years, will, in the age that is now dawning, demonstrate their beneficence and their power; and the marvel will be, that the ignorance and brutality of man could have so long succeeded in suppressing them. It is true, even yet, that among otherwise intelligent persons the majority do not believe that any such Fountain of Knowledge has ever existed. They are looking alone to the future, and waiting, and they hail with delight every new discovery in science for the betterment of man. It will be for all such the greatest of all discoveries that "to go back to Plato is to make progress," and that the Egyptian, Chaldean, and Hindoo Mysteries had, ages ago, exhausted all philosophies, apprehended all sciences, and recorded their priceless treasures of wisdom in glyph and allegory for the benefit of the latest generations of the human race. By and by, even our scientists will, like weary and disappointed children, become tired in trying to do it all over again by themselves, and then they will no longer turn a deaf ear to the Immortal, though silent, Voices of the Past. But how, some one may ask, were the Ancients, even before the dawn of what we call history, enabled to make such transcendent discoveries? If, in the preceding chapter, the present author has succeeded in presenting even a faint outline of the meaning of the word Master, and what Initiation really accomplishes, the inquirer will not have far to seek for an answer to his question. The Secret Doctrine declares that it is the result, not of the vain guesses, or the tortuous investigations of ignorant men, but of the recorded and carefully tested experiences of generation after generation of trained Adepts and Perfect Masters, the Advance-guards of Humanity in every age. Things are not true because they are old, but old because they are true. Immortality belongs to Truth and not to error. A thing is not true because God hath said it, or is *supposed* to have said it; God said it *because it is true;* and the whole manifestation of Nature is thus the uttered word of divinity. The Master who is *at-one* with both Nature and Divinity discerns the truth, and teaches and records it for all future generations of men. But it is only in an age of freedom and enlightenment that the voice of the Master can be heard; but it should be ever remembered that the sole authority of the Master is in the Truth; and not the authority of Truth in the

Master. Just here lies the distinction between Religion and Superstition. The masses will ever seek a sign, but the one only sign of the Master is his service to humanity. "He who can best work and best agree" is called a Master. Service and Harmony: these are the sign-manuals of the real Initiate. The Ignorant may worship as a god him who can produce signs and wonders, and when weary of worship return to wallow in the mire, forgetful of the miracle. Hence the real Masters in all ages have avoided publicity — "gone into a mountain apart" — and shunned the applause of men, preferring to be despised and slandered rather than have the truth ignored, and be themselves glorified of men.

[1] Morals and Dogma, p. 734.   [2] Morals and Dogma, p. 842.

Chapter Eight - The Great Lodge

The profound secrecy surrounding the Ancient Mysteries, and the obligation of secrecy imposed upon every initiate into the Masonic Fraternity arise from many causes, and varying conditions, some of which have already been pointed out. In times of political oppression and ecclesiastical persecution it became necessary to conceal the identity of all members of secret fraternities; and, as far as possible, the principles of the order were also concealed for mutual protection. When to be known as a Mason or an Occultist was to be hunted down like a criminal, to be imprisoned for life, or perhaps to be tortured and burned, men naturally concealed their connection with the Lodge, or their interest in the Secret Doctrine. There is probably no degree in Masonry today that has not been invaded by members of religious orders like the Jesuits. Those who are familiar with the principles of these Sodalities are well aware that under the plea that "the end justifies the means," no member of these bodies would hesitate to take any obligation imposed, in order to possess himself of a coveted secret that might support the power and maintain the prerogative of his Sodality, knowing in advance that absolution for the crime of perjury in violating his sacred obligation would not only be assured him, but that he would be applauded and perhaps canonized for his zeal and his devotion to religion, as many a Saint in the calendar has been canonized in the past upon far less "Saintly" grounds.

In the face of all so-called exposures, and all betrayal, Masonry pursues the even tenor of its way, and tyles its lodges as carefully, and inculcates its obligation of secrecy just as though apostasy were impossible, and perjury a crime unknown to the code of civilized communities. Notwithstanding all so-called exposures, it would be exceeding hazardous for any one, except a regularly initiated Brother, to attempt to gain admission to the Lodge; and no possible motive can be assigned why any honest man should desire to receive the rites and benefits of the Lodge except in the order and under the conditions prescribed. But after all other reasons assigned for the secrecy of the Lodge, probably the tradition that such was always the rule in the mysteries, has had more to do with concealment than anything else; and the real reason for concealment in the mysteries has been herein previously shown to be on account of the power that attaches to the real knowledge possessed by the Master. The penalties imposed for violating the solemn obligations voluntarily taken, may, at times, have been literally executed by the agents of the Lodge in medieval or pre-Christian times; but in modern times these awful penalties have undoubtedly been substituted by "the excration of all honest men and Masons." In genuine initiations into the really occult mysteries, the penalties for unworthiness in any and all directions consisted in the apostate becoming the victim of the powers he had himself invoked. He had created a Frankenstein which he was no longer able to control, and it destroyed him. Hence, the warning was true and necessary, but the real method of its execution was disguised, except that it was portrayed as terrible. Too little is known as yet in the West of genuine occultism, to make further explanation intelligible. All space, and every plane of nature is full of Life and Intelligence, and Bulwer's "Demon of the Threshold" may be neither a joke nor a romance, as many cases of obscession recorded in the annals of Medicine and Spiritualism abundantly prove. The "Principalities and Powers of the Air," of which the Apostle speaks, and of which the Kabalah treats very fully, are the Elementals described, though but blindly, in ancient occult literature. When the real nature of obscession is understood, and the character of these depraved entities becomes known, it will be discerned how little is to be gained, and how much is to be risked by invoking them. Here lies the reason why mediumship should be discouraged and regarded as a disease, or, at best, a misfortune. Real Seership is a very different thing indeed from obscession in any form. If Seership be compared to the Ecstasy of an innocent and happy child, obscession may be likened to the delirium of drunkenness or madness.

Some idea may be gained, perhaps, from the foregoing of the source and character of the penalty for the violation of obligations assumed by the Neophite in the mysteries. In the "Mystery of Cloomber," Conan Doyle portrays the *"idea,"* but makes the execution of the penalty at once fantastic, horrible, and impossible. No real Master, even such as he portrays, could ever play the bungling part of executioner, such as he depicts, but would leave the criminal to the snares and devices of his own creation. The imagination of the novelist can hardly supply the philosophy of true occultism.

The stories that have come down to us of the magnificent pageantry, and the almost superhuman trials attending initiation into the Mysteries, from those of ancient Egypt down to Tom Moore's Epicurean, all pertained to the various degrees of the Lesser Mysteries. The secrets of the Greater Mysteries were never written or told. What they were can only be surmised from a complete philosophical knowledge of what initiation really means, and some idea as to what the last supreme revelation may be. This has probably never been betrayed in any individual case, nor is it likely that it will ever be revealed, because, as shown in the preceding chapters, it is the meeting face to face with one's own god; the Higher Self, latent in every man, but now wholly revealed. It concerns the things "impossible to utter," of St. Paul, an Initiate. The philosophy of the whole process may, however, be fairly apprehended as the consummation of the Higher Evolution of Man. Thus philosophy, for him who can understand it, takes the place of the whole of the instruction of the Lesser Mysteries, except such practical experience and final training of the neophite as enable him to enter the Greater Mysteries. So far as mere teaching is concerned, or the apprehension of what is to be done, and how, philosophy is the teacher, and is better fitted to the present intellectual age than any other form of instruction. When a genuine School for the Revival of the Lost Mysteries of Antiquity is established, worthy and well-qualified neophytes will doubtless receive not only instruction, but practical training.

Hitherto in this work hints,, outlines, suggestions, and running comments or relations only have been given; and every intelligent reader must have observed the difficulty of describing that which was never intended to be revealed.

We may now undertake to give a diagram or a picture of an idea running through all history like a theme in a musical composition. The idea crops out here and there in history, but it is not history for reasons already made clear. The full-page diagram (see Frontispiece) is a Symbol of the Secret Doctrine, and some of its principal ramifications and seats. Like all symbols, it is not the thing symbolized; and, as already declared, it is not a history of the Great Lodge and the Secret Doctrine. If it should by and by be shown that the Great Lodge, historically, had its first seat in Egypt, or in Ethiopia, which is possible, instead of in Old India, or in Ireland, which is not impossible, or on the Continent of Atlantis, which is more likely still, it would not make any difference with our diagram, which, as already repeatedly declared, is not designed to represent history, but *the influence of an Idea* upon the Civilizations and Religions of the world. When the true and complete history of what are called the British Druids is written, the legends of the now "Unhappy Emerald Island" will be deciphered, and the beautiful legend of Venus rising from the Foam of the Sea will not be the most grand or beautiful of Ireland's stories.

On the scientific presumption that every effect must have had an adequate cause, we have the right to assume that the Landmarks of Masonry, and the traditions of the Secret Doctrine, are not without foundation in fact. Furthermore: the further back we go in history, and beyond history, the grander become the monuments of the Secret Science. Pythagoras and Plato found all their knowledge ready-made in the Egyptian and Babylonian Mysteries. The deeper we delve into the past the grander become these Ancient Monuments. The Zodiac and the Pyramids alone, by the knowledge they betray of Astronomy, Mechanics, Mathematics and Architecture, demonstrate the existence of a science in pre-historic times such as we moderns have not yet been able to imitate, or even to read. We are like miners following a vein of gold in a crevasse of the rocks. Precious ore crops out here and there, and is again concealed; it grows richer as we proceed, till the conviction becomes irresistible that deep in the bowels of the earth, or beneath some mountain range, there must be a great "pocket," the real source of all this buried treasure. The analogy is complete, and the reasoning scientific. But if the ancient monuments on the physical plane are unimpeachable, and those in the heavens unapproachable, they are still more transcendent in the Intellectual and Spiritual realms. There is not a religion, a science, or a philosophy, known to man, that cannot be traced back to Old India; with this difference, however, that we have only the fragments, the broken columns, or the disjointed images of a complete and perfect structure as it once existed. The oldest books or written records known to us today, such as The Egyptian Ritual of the Dead, and the hymns of the Vedas, have scarcely yet been spelled out by their letters. Such translations as have been given us are both superficial and literal, and the inner meaning, always expressed in symbols, seldom appears at all. The interpretation that has heretofore been put upon them by Philologists, few of whom can rank as Symbologists, and not one of whom in Europe is a real Occultist, is that they are the crude imaginings of a primitive people who knew nothing of science, and who were devoted to superstition. These translators have achieved fame as "Great Orientalists," and they have undoubtedly done a great work in introducing ancient languages to modern times, and in doing their best to interpret ancient belief, but in nearly all instances these orientalists have been biased by the traditions and false lights of modern Christendom. In another chapter of this work it has been shown what infinite pains has been taken by ignorant Monks, and by zealous Ecclesiastics, to obliterate these ancient records, and to deface them by interpolations and forgeries in order that the Christian records and traditions might stand unchallenged. The best of our Orientalists are, even unconsciously, influenced by the results that have been thus achieved. When Western students are capable of apprehending, and ready to receive the true interpretation of the ancient symbolism, it is possible that native scholars who not only know Sanskrit, but who are thoroughly familiar with the Secret Doctrine, may be found to enlighten them.

Take a single instance. The Atomic Theory, known to have been more or less familiar to certain ancient Greek writers, has made great progress in Modern science. But in no form conceived byModern science — and the forms have been many and contradictory, has this theory proved competent to account for all of the phenomena observed. It has remained for us, therefore, still an Hypothesis and not a Law. The Atoms of Modern Science, whether conceived as solid, rluidic, gaseous, or etheric, — for they have been imagined to be all of these — are, nevertheless, regarded as *dead atoms*. Even when conceived as mere neutral centers, or "mathematical points," they are still far removed from Life or Intelligence. Leibnitz conceived them as Monads, each a living mirror of the Universe, every Monad reflecting every other. "Compare these views," says a modern writer, "with that in certain Sanskrit Slokas translated by Sir William Jones, in which it is said that the creative source of the Divine Mind." ... "Hidden in a veil of thick darkness, *formed mirrors of the atoms* of the world, and *cast reflection from its own face on every atom*." When we have learned more of Radiant Matter, and the Roentgen Ray, we shall have come far nearer this old Atomic Theory, and Matter will no longer be regarded as "dead and inert."

The Hymns of the Vedas were doubtless the original allegorical form of the Secret Doctrine, and the Rishis — called "gods," but really Sublime and Perfect Masters — were their creators.

Antedating the Vedas, then, was the Great Lodge of Adepts, who created the Religion, inspired the Civilization, and taught the profound Science that made old India great. If only traditions and broken monuments remain, these still outrank all modern achievements of man. The ancient government was Patriarchal; the Ruler was also a Master Initiate, and the people were regarded as his children. In those ancient days a Reigning Prince considered it not beneath his dignity to go into the desert alone, and sit at the feet of some inspired recluse, in order that he might receive more light, which he would again dispense to his people. Instead of teaching superstition and idolatry, when the real meaning of the Vedic symbolism is revealed, it will, perhaps, be found to be the thinnest veil ever imposed between the Sublime Wisdom and the apprehension of men. The old' gods were the symbolical or personified attributes of Nature, through which man was taught to apprehend the existence of the Supreme Spirit. This was not Polytheism, nor Idolatry, but a system of teaching that which could not be altogether defined, and of pointing to that which must forever remain unknown, and Unknowable, by the aid of symbol, parable, and allegory. No word-painting known to man seems half so beautiful as some of these ancient parables and allegories. Not only was every oblation of love and duty portrayed, and every joy of home and affection illustrated, and the most common duties of life, feats of valor, devotion, and self-sacrifice depicted, but in a language so musical, and in rhythm and meter so perfect, as to make the whole recital more like a symphony than a poem. The whole composition was a mantram. On nearly every page of the Anugita it is said — in relation to this or that — "they relate this ancient story, in the form of a dialogue, which occurred" — so and so.

If India today is like an old woman in her dotage, and her Priests have turned Harpies to devour her remaining spiritual life, the record of primeval greatness can never be dimmed or destroyed.

In the olden time the Brahman was indeed "twice-born," and it was the *second birth* alone that made him Brahman. The parables, then, were not invented to conceal the truth from those who could apprehend it, or to keep the people in ignorance in order that the Priests or Ruler might preserve their power. Power came not from the people, but from the possession of supreme knowledge, and this knowledge, continually exercised and exemplified, was the badge of office and the sign of authority. To such a Priesthood the people rendered most willing obedience. The doors of Initiation were open to all who had evolved the capacity to "Know, to Dare, to Do, and to Keep Silent," in regard to that which should not be prematurely revealed.

With the light of the Great Lodge standing in the midst, the Religion of the people was a perfect representative of Science and Philosophy, in which superstition and idolatry found no place, hence the symmetry in our diagram of the old Wisdom-Religion.

The religion of India being thus inspired by the Great Lodge was expressed in the Hymns of the Vedas. This was the old Brahmanism, the Religion of Brahm; the Father-Mother of All.

But in time the Priesthood became corrupt; the people forsook the ancient worship. Then came Chrisna, and later Buddha, to restore that which was lost. The Brahmins, now no longer "twice-born," but a priestly caste, jealous of power, since they were no longer real Masters, arose in rebellion, and the mission of Buddha largely failed in India, and found its principal converts in Ceylon, in distant lands, and the isles of the sea.

The religions of Egypt and Chaldea had back of them the same Secret Doctrine, or Mysteries; and they were also both Scientific and Philosophical. But Egypt and Chaldea repeated the folly of India, and perished with the degradation of their religions. Traditions of the Secret Doctrine still existed, and Masters like Hermes, Zoroaster, Confucius, and Laotse appeared in different lands from time to time to revive the old religion under new names, and often under a different form of symbolism. Pythagoras and the Schools of the Persian Maji for many centuries kept the true light burning. The conquest of Egypt by Cambyses, as already referred to, completed the ruin of the land of the Pharaohs, and Pythagoras and Plato became the links between the old philosophy and the Christian Era, together with the Jewish Kabalah, derived jointly from the Mysteries of Egypt and Chaldea, though more largely, perhaps, from the latter.

From the Essenes, the Schools of Alexandria, then in all their glory, from the Kabalah and the philosophy of Plato, the Christian mysteries were derived. During the first three centuries of our era these doctrines flourished; but were finally crushed by the conquests of Constantine, and then came the dark ages.

The Religion of Jesus was in every respect that of the Mysteries; it was the same old Wisdom-Religion, though the ethical features were more pronounced, as being most needed among what was called "a generation of vipers," and a "stiff-necked and rebellious people." The ethical teachings of Jesus in time give place to Priestcraft and Sacerdotalism; to worldly power, and conquest; and the religion of Constantine was finally replaced by the "Holy Inquisition," a religion of torture and bloodshed.

The Sufis, among the conquering Mohammedans, knew the Secret Science, but their power paled in the presence of the "Sword of the Prophet."

Freemasonry, though not a lineal descendant of the ancient mysteries, may justly be regarded as a connecting link between the ancient wisdom and modern times. While imitating many of the ancient rites and ceremonies, and preserving many of the ancient landmarks, and transmitting to modern times a *Grand Ideal,* Masonry stands as one of the greatest benefactors of the present age. If it has preserved only the broken fragments of ancient grandeur, it has, nevertheless, cherished and honored these as a priceless inheritance. Will Masons really undertake the noble and glorious work of rebuilding the City and Temple of the Lord? Will they unite to restore the primeval wisdom and glory? Will they search diligently among the rubbish for the "Stone that the Builders rejected," [1] and for the "Lost Word of the Master"? Alas! who can say? There is another link to our chain of evidence and line of transmission. The grips, signs, and passwords, by which a Mason recognizes a Brother, pertain to the Lesser Mysteries. The real Master knows his fellows by other signs. It has been elsewhere shown that the true Adept is both clairvoyant and clairaudient. There is a magnetic atmosphere, or radiation, around every human being, and, indeed, something of the kind around every animal and every inanimate object. Every one feels this magnetic aura when coming in contact with others, even though they may see nothing, and may often be unconscious of its effects. This atmosphere of the individual is the source of what is called "Sympathy," and "Antipathy;" or attraction, and repulsion. It is not imaginary, but real. It is the focalized result of individual character, and contains all the potencies and qualities of the individual's life. It is composed of matter, is magnetic, has a definite mode of motion, and definite color. It may be absorbed by or transmitted to another. The vibrations incident to it are the co-ordinate result of the combined and varying activities of the Principles in man. The Key-note in every individual is thus determined as a scientific fact in matter. In the sensualist, and in all who are degraded by passion and selfishness, the color of this aura is red, like the comb of a cock; and the sensation which it produces upon the sensitive and pure is often described as hot and Stirling. In an individual who is unselfish and pure-minded, the color may alternate between a golden yellow and blue, and the effect described by the sensitive is that it is cool, restful, and inspiring.

If the foregoing is true, and it is easily verified, and if a real Master is able to see all of these conditions which are usually invisible to others, he would hardly need to depend upon "grips, signs, or passwords" to recognize a Fellow. Man betrays his character, his heredity, his ideals, and all his past life in every lineament of his face, in the contour and pose of his body, in his gait, in his handwriting, in the lines in his hand, in the tones of his voice, in the expression of the eye; in short, no man *possesses* character. Character is that which he altogether is, and not something apart from himself. One need not be a Master to discover all this; he needs only to observe, to think, and to reason on what he sees. In even the ordinary walks of life the Artist, the Musician, the Mechanic, all recognize their fellows by signs that are familiar and unfailing. It can hardly be imagined that in the higher science, and in the case of the deeper student or Adept, the signs of character should be less pronounced or less plain, or that the Adept, possessed of far finer senses and a wider range of knowledge, should fail in interpreting them. The individual who is really sincere and devout will not fail to recognize sincerity and true devotion in an acquaintance or in any character in history that possessed these virtues. Hence it is that the Student of the Sacred Science or Occultism, though not himself an Adept, learns to recognize by unfailing signs those in the present or in the past who really know the true wisdom. Its signs and symbols are not the stolen Shibboleths by which the real student can be betrayed. Every Mason knows enough of the picture language or Art Speech to be able to speak of many things in the presence of others without revealing the secrets of the Lodge. Even the criminal classes have their dialects or *patois*.

History is full of pretenders in Occultism. Pretension alone is a sign of ignorance, and the proposition to "sell the truth" is always a sign of fraud. There are, however, many names in history that have been covered with obloquy, and their possessors charged with fraud and imposition, who were, nevertheless, genuine Adepts, if not Perfect Masters. We must distinguish between self-conviction that comes from the pretender's own mouth and those accusations that come from others and are unsupported by evidence. The pretender is often loaded with honors and found rolling in wealth, as the reward of deceit and lying, of fraud and corruption, which he is shrewd enough to conceal. On the other hand, the real Master is often gibbeted by the populace and anathematized by the church, because he is neither time-serving nor willing to barter the truth for gold.

All along the line of history may be found those who possessed the true light. Concealing both their wisdom and their own identity from vulgar notice and foolish praise, they have walked the earth unseen and unknown to the many, but always known to their fellows, and to all real seekers after true wisdom. The ignorance of the rabble, the zeal of the superstitious, and the "Vicegerent of God" have often made sad inroads among the servants of the Great Lodge; yet they have never been altogether exterminated; they have always existed to bear witness; and *they exist today!* If the reader is ready to deny all this, of course it can make no difference to the real Adept, and it is certainly a matter of indifference to the present writer. One can do no more than to state candidly what he believes, and to set forth that which he knows to be true.

These Adepts, or Masters, have, in every age, constituted the Great Lodge. Whether they congregate beneath vaulted domes, or meet at stated times, no one would be likely to know unless he belonged to the same degree; but one thing is very certain, and that is, that they bring help and knowledge to the world when most needed, and they are working thus today in the West as they have not done before for many weary centuries. They are enabled to work now, because the ground has been prepared for them by *"one who knew,"* and who served them to the death in the face of scorn and slander. They have been aided also by many ignorant but faithful believers in their existence, and in their work, who have been rewarded at every step by "More-Light." Almost coincident with the close of the present century is the close of a great cycle: namely, the first cycle of five thousand years of the Kali Yuga. Aside from unusual astronomical conjunctions, many perturbations in space, earthquakes, cyclones, and tidal waves, there are also predicted great social upheavals, political changes, and both mental and physical epidemics. In other words, as is already apparent to all who read the signs of the times, the present is a transition period, and whatever influences are to mold the coming century must begin their operations at the present time. This is therefore the seed-time, and the harvest will be by and by.

Note — Many references in literature might be adduced giving accounts of the existence of the Great Lodge. Two of these may here be mentioned, viz., that given in the Life of Apollonius Tyanaeus of his visit to the Adepts of India, and the account of Flamel and the Adepts in an old book called Hermippus Redivivus, by Campbell. The present object is, however, rather to unfold a philosophy than to gather facts; to explain what a Master may be, rather than to point out their abodes.

[1] See Plate IX.

Chapter Nine - An Outline of Symbolism

A man standing by a horizontally revolving wheel might be taken as a symbol of every vessel made of clay, whether for honor or dishonor. Every detail of ornament or of shape might hold a legend, an allegory, or a parable; or indicate a use; but the *Potter at his wheel* would be a universal and allincluding symbol; a pictorial expression of creative thought in man. The Chinese written-language is nothing more than symbolical writing, each of its several thousand letters being a symbol. This pictorial expression of an idea or a thought, this Art-speech, is Symbolism. When the symbols are of familiar things, and as various as human experience, the knowledge conveyed is common. When the symbols are few and simple, whether commonplace or grotesque, like a point, a circle or a square, or a dragon, or a man with horns, the knowledge conveyed is not for the masses, but for him alone who holds the key. Take the following simple series: a point •, a circle **0**, a point within a circle ⊙; the circle horizontally divided ⊖; the lower half again divided ⊕; the upper half divided ⊖; a cross within the circle ⊕; the cross alone ⊤+⊥; and we have the series emanating from the point and the circle. If, now, any process in Nature can be found to unfold in the same orderly manner, then any one of the series of symbols would be found to symbolize a definite stage in the process of nature. Hence, the meaning of the symbol would expand, just in proportion as one's knowledge of the natural process increased. If nature's planes are seven, and each plane sevenfold, there would come to be groups of symbols pertaining to each plane, and a key to each group. Take, for example, the symbol ⊖. Aside from the philosophical meaning as the third in the series (O⊙⊖) of Mother-Nature within Infinitude, it represents a universal law of proportion, and the exact mathematical ratio of the circumference to its diameter throughout nature; applicable alike to the circle of a pinhead or a sun. Here then would be a symbol in Mathematics or Geometry, correlating Space and Time with Form and Proportion. Such a symbol would, however, have little meaning except to the philosopher or the Mathematician. To the latter the Greek π, or the proportion 1:314159, or to the Kabalistic 113:355, would at once recall the original symbol and the whole series. If, in addition, our Mathematician knew the different ratios of vibration incident to the three planes of evolution represented by O⊙⊖, he would have the key to occult physics, and could forecast results, measure effects, and induce changes beyond the ordinary plane of crude matter.

The simple series to which I have referred will illustrate the whole science of symbolism.

Added to this science of Symbolism there is an Archaic Art-Speech, by the use of which a double meaning is given to language, so that the most ordinary form of speech may be used to convey a deep scientific or philosophical meaning. This gives rise to the allegory and parable, the outer form of which may convey to the ignorant a lesson in ethics, and to the learned a principle in science. The most complicated form of this symbolism and Art-Speech known to modern times is, perhaps, the Jewish Kabalah, from which most of the glyphs of Freemasonry are derived. The object of the present work is not to explain all these symbols, for that would require a volume of symbolism, and have but little value when written except to the curious.

Perhaps the most familiar symbol of a Mason is the Square and Compass, found in every Lodge, and worn as a badge of fraternal recognition. We are told in the Lodge that the Square is an instrument with which the practical Mason measures and lays out his work, but we as free and accepted Masons are taught to make use of it for the more noble and glorious purpose of squaring our conduct with the golden rule, with principles of right and justice, etc. So also with the Compass; the practical use is made symbolical of the higher moral obligation, to circumscribe our desires and keep our passions within due bounds. But Masonry is "a system of Morals illustrated by Symbols," and *something more;* and there is hence a science and a philosophy concealed in the symbolism of the square and compass. This may be outlined as follows: The Square with its one right angle and its scale of measurements applies to surfaces and solids, and deals with the apparently fixed states of matter. It represents solidarity, symmetry and proportion; and this involves the sciences of arithmetic and geometry. The Compass with movable angle set in the Lodge at an angle of 60°, applies to the circle and the sphere; to movements and revolutions. In a general sense, the square is a symbol of matter, and the earth; the Compass, of Spirit and the heavens. In the Lodge the square and compass cross each other, and this fact is made a symbol of progression, from the degree of Entered Apprenticeship to that of Master. The compass is set at an angle of 60°, and is representative of the movements of Spirit, and, if crossed at a certain distance from the angle, will produce an equilateral triangle; the three angles and the three sides equal, it now represents perfect equilibrium, or proportion. [1]

"For the Apprentice, the points of the compass are beneath the Square. For the Fellowcraft, one is above and one beneath. For the Master, both are dominant, and have rule, control and empire over the symbol of the earthly and material. [2]

If the reader now refers to what was said in a previous chapter concerning the descent of Spirit into matter, and the First Trinity represented by a triangle; Matter, Force and Spirit (Law); and in Man — Manas, Buddhi and Atma; he will readily see that the compass may fairly represent this primary trinity, concealed under the square of matter, till by progression it emerges, and finally, in the Master's hands, gains dominion over matter. In the man of ignorance (sin), the spirit is concealed, and the body and its passions hold dominion. This is the state of the Neophite, or Entered-Apprentice. In the Fellowcraft's degree, the symbols are interlaced; and in the Master's, Matter is subordinated to Spirit. The lectures on the several degrees explain the method by which the Compass (Spirit) may gain dominion over the Square (body and passion) through the greater activity of Spirit, "in circumscribing our desires, and keeping our passions within due bounds." The perfect equilibrium of spirit and matter is symbolized by the six-pointed star, [3] which is again only another form of the Square and Compass, each now having a baseline from which to form a triangle. Inclose the star in a circle, which symbolizes Infinity, and you symbolize the harmony, or at-one-ment of the Spirit that descended, and the body, now purified, with Divinity, or the Over-Soul. Place within the Star thus inclosed the Egyptian emblem of Life, ☥, and we symbolize *Immortality,* as the result of regeneration. Transform the circle into a serpent and it now symbolizes Wisdom, as the crown or result of equilibrium; and is also a double glyph of the return of

matter to its source in spirit. Separate the tongue and tail of the serpent by a *Thor's Hammer,* or Svastica, inclosed within a circle, and it symbolizes regeneration through conquest of animal sense, precisely as taught in the Lodge, under the spiritual meaning of the symbol of the Compass.

"Freemasonry is the subjugation of the Human that is in man, by the Divine; the conquest of the Appetites and Passions, by the Moral Sense and Reason; a continual effort, struggle, and warfare of the Spiritual against the Material and Sensual. That victory, when it has been achieved and secured, and the conqueror may rest upon his shield and wear the well-earned laurels, is the True Holy Empire."

The Masonic Apron made of lambskin symbolizes innocence or purity, the condition required of candidates in all real initiation. [4] The shape of the apron is that of a perfect square surmounted by a triangle. We have here the three and the four, making seven; the triangle representing spirit, the square representing matter; the triangle representing the threefold attributes of the One; the square representing the four elements. As spirit, the triangle represents, or is symbolized by, heat, light and flame.

The Entered Apprentice starts on his career with the triangle surmounting the square (spirit has not yet descended into matter). As he progresses the descent takes place, and we have the triangle in the square, as heretofore illustrated; and finally as a Master the ascent of the square into the triangle begins, which every Master Mason will understand. Masonry being a "progressive science," the progress of the neophite is thus made to conform to the process of evolution and the descent of spirit into matter, and this is illustrated by the manner in which he is taught to wear his apron in each degree in the Blue Lodge. The Entered Apprentice is not only a "hewer of wood and a drawer of water," but he is a novice, taking his first instruction, and this is symbolized by his apron.

The tradition of the Master's Word, of the power which its possession gives to the Master; the story of its loss and the search for its recovery; the tradition of the Ineffable Name in connection with the Lost Word, showing that it could not or should not be pronounced, except with bated breath; or, as the Hindoo tradition declares, "with the hand covering the mouth." The symbolism of the three greater and three lesser lights, and the play made in many places on the word *Light* itself, in conjunction with the Lost Word, all these references and uses constitute a complicated Symbolism working in and toward a common center or glyph, which, taken in conjunction with the building and restoration of the Temple, constitute the secret Symbolism of Masonry, and illustrate the whole process of Initiation. What real initiation is has been outlined in a previous chapter. These symbols, when correctly interpreted, serve two purposes. First: they reveal a complete philosophy of the Creation of the Universe and of Man, unfolding all essences, powers, and potencies, and their mutual relations and correlations. Second: they unfold the process of Initiation as synonymous with the uninterrupted evolution of man guided by knowledge and design along the lines of least resistance. In the third degree the candidate impersonates *Hiram,* who has been shown to be identical with the *Christos* of the Greeks, and with the Sun-Gods of all other nations. The superiority of Masonry at this point over all exoteric Religions consists in this: All these religions take the symbol for the thing symbolized. Christ was originally *like* the Father. Now He is made *identical* with the Father. [5] In deifying Jesus the whole of humanity is bereft of *Christos* as an eternal potency within every human soul, a latent Christ in every man. In thus deifying one man, they have orphaned the whole of humanity! On the other hand, Masonry, in making every candidate personify *Hiram,* has preserved the original teaching, which is a universal glyph. Few candidates may be aware that Hiram whom they have represented and personified is ideally and precisely the same as Christ. Yet such is undoubtedly the case. This old philosophy shows what Christ as a glyph means, and how the Christ-state results from real Initiation, or from the evolution of the human into the Divine. Regeneration is thus given a meaning that is both apprehensible and attainable; both philosophical and scientific; and at once ideal and practical. In the Tetragrammaton, or four-lettered name of Deity, the Greek followers of Pythagoras found a glyph by which they both expressed and concealed their philosophy, and it is the Hebrew tetrad IHVH, or "Yod, hé, vau, hé," that is introduced into Masonry with the Pythagorean art speech. The devout Hebrew, in reading the sacred Text, when he came to the tetrad IHVH, substituted the word *Adonai* (Lord), and if the word was written with the points of Alhim, he called it *Elohom.* This custom is preserved in Masonry by giving the candidate a substitute for the Master's Word. The Hebrew tetrad "Yod, hé, vau, hé," is produced by repeating the "hé." The root word is a triad, and the quaternary is undoubtedly a blind. The Sacred word is found in the mysteries as a binary, a trinary, and a quaternary; as with the Hindoos we have the om, and the aum, indicating different methods of pronouncing the Sacred name. The Pythagorean Tetraktys is represented by numbers, 1, 2, 3, 4 = 10, and by points or "Yods" in the form of a triangle; [6] this is called the "lesser tetraktys," while a triangle composed of eight rows in the same form and containing thirty-six "Yods," or points, is called the "greater Tetraktys." This corresponds to the three lesser lights, and three greater lights of the. Blue Lodge, though the monitorial explanations in' the lodge are, to say the least, incomplete. In the Pythagorean philosophy both the lesser and greater tetraktys are represented by equilateral triangles, and the points, in either case, form the angles of a series of lesser triangles. In the lesser tetraktys these triangles are altogether nine, or three times three. In the greater they count forty-nine, or seven times seven; and in each case the series runs, from apex to base, 1, 3, 5, for the lesser, and 1, 3, 5, 7, 9, 11, 13, for the greater tetraktys, or by a series of odd numbers; while the points, before the triangles are formed, run consecutively, 1, 2, 3, 4, 5, 6, 7, 8. These symbols were thus used as "odd" and "even," to carry a philosophical meaning, and to illustrate the doctrine of Emanation.

In the Pythagorean system Spirit is everywhere represented as the Universal. "All multitude must necessarily issue from One," and that one is Spirit. All emanations and subdivisions must therefore be related to the One by absolute geometry (perfect forms) and absolute mathematics (perfect numbers and movements).

In the 47th Problem, so famous in ancient philosophy (see Plate XI), and far older than Pythagoras or Euclid, we have a symbol of the perfect proportions between number and forms; between spirit and matter; and between universals and particulars; and this is a constant symbol in Masonic Lodges.

In the Pythagorean Triangle, or tetrad (see Plate V), this same philosophy is symbolized.

Proposition

"Subdivide a regular figure in such a manner that the subdivisions shall be the same shape as the figure, and 16 in number, and with 4 of the subdivisions bounding each side of the figure: 16 is the square of 4, or the Tetraktys. *The triangle series is of odd numbers; the square even. The ten "Yods" occupy all the upright triangle divisions."* (Quoted, with plate, from print by Fred. G. Plummer.)

This Pythagorean method of "philosophizing according to numbers" has not only fallen into disuse in modern times, but has often been deemed altogether fanciful and been subject to ridicule, simply because the philosophy upon which it is based is lost. It originally constituted the Art-Speech, or glyphs, in which that philosophy was expressed, and to understand the one is to recover the other. This philosophy bridged the gap between mind and matter through apprehension of the one underlying Law. It connected Physics with Metaphysics through the Science of Mathematics, or the relations of Number to Form, or of Equilibrium tomotion. The Adept knew the relations between the movements (vibrations) that produce thought, those that produce form, those that produce color, and those that produce light and sound, and the number of these in each case. The source of all these is a Trinity; the form of emanation a septenary. Hence the play upon the formula "three times three" and "seven times seven." The first postulate of this philosophy has been shown in a previous chapter to be Abstract Space, and Abstract, absolute Motion; and this absolute motion is that of the Primordial Atoms, thus constituting "the center which is everywhere and the circumference which is nowhere;" *i.e.,* fills all space. It is necessary, however, to remind the reader that these "Atoms" are not those of modern Science, or those that compose what we call Matter, for the reason that they are, one and all, endowed (potentially) with Consciousness, Life, and Intelligence, and are equally world-builders and man-builders. They are the vehicles and the basis of all Law in Nature. They form alike the moving panorama of thought and the tides of the restless sea: The beating of the human heart, and the revolutions of Suns and Solar Systems; the breath of an infant, and the "Breath of Brahm." There is universal and eternal Unity and Equilibrium in the midst of universal diversity; Perpetual Involution of Spirit or essence, and endless evolution of form and variety; and back of all, the One Eternal Principle, unknown and forever unknowable, without beginning, without end, without change. Space is the mantle that forever conceals Him. Abstract, absolute Motion is his Fiat. Creation is His Logos, Word, Speech, Expression, Will, Thought — call it what you will. Man is a "Spark" from this "Flame," and, in the last analysis, as incomprehensible to himself as God. This Spark of Divinity in man is his consciousness, and this in a previous chapter we have postulated as a fact, nothing more.

This brings us to the origin of the Tetraktys, the origin of the Ineffable Name, the Lost Word. The Hebrews seem to have derived their Tetraktys from the Chaldo-Egyptian Mysteries, and these may be traced to the Zoroastrian Fire Philosophy, till finally the Word is A. U. M.. In both Persian or Zend and in Sanscrit, the three letters are found in many names that designate fire, flame, Spirit, essence, etc. This again is a glyph or form of expression. Every emanation is a trinity; and Fire, Flame, and Light are the most perfect synthesis of this tri-unity. Consider the expressions, "The Lord is a consuming fire;" "Since God is light, and never but in unapproached Light dwelt from eternity," etc.

The symbol is found in all Scriptures, but only in the Mysteries was the meaning thus symbolized made known. Here, then, is the origin of all the *trinities* found in Masonry, the plainest of which are the trinities of Light, and the most superficial explanations are found connected with the three lesser Lights of the Lodge.

"The Primitive Holy Symbol, composed of three letters, in which the Vedic Triad is comprehended, ought to be kept secret like another Triple Veda. He who knows the mystic value of this syllable, knows the Veda." — *Laws of Manu, Book XI,* No. 265.

"The mortal who raws nigh unto fire will have a light from Divinity." — *Chaldean Oracle.*

"In every world shines forth a Triad, whereof the Principle is Unity." — *Chaldean Oracle.*

"It is necessary to know that the Divine Name of its indwelling Potency, and which is a symbol of the impression of the Demiourgos, according to which it does not go forth from its being, is ineffable and Secret, and known only to the Gods themselves." — *Proclus.*

The legend of the Lost Word and the Potency of the Ineffable Name are inseparable. They are the glyphs of Paradise Lost, and Paradise Regained; or of the Fall and the Redemption of man. So also is the legend of re-building the temple, a glyph of Initiation, which is the same as Regeneration and Evolution.

This ancient Wisdom belongs in a special sense to Masonry, for it has done most of any organization of modern times to preserve the ancient landmarks, and has honored and protected the sacred symbols. If Masonry has made only a superficial use of these hoary secrets, and their deeper meaning is still unknown to the craft, it is equally unknown to all others, except as the result of genuine initiation. One may know that a thing exists, where it is to be found, and that it is above all price, without knowing, to the last analysis, what it is. Such is the secret to the Lost Word, or the Ineffable Name. Its secret lies in exact vibrations under mathematical and synchronous relations; and its Law is Equilibrium, or Eternal Harmony.

[1] Radius of circle and chord of arc equal.
[2] Morals and Dogma, p. 854.
[3] See plate VII.
[4] See Plate XII.
[5] Here lies the true meaning of Abiff, "of, or from my Father." Hiram = Christos, and Abiff = "at one with the Father," i. e., "of," or "from."
[6] See Plates V and VIII.

Chapter Ten - Conclusion

The foregoing pages can justly be called fragments only of the Secret Doctrine and of the Symbols of Freemasonry. A systematic treatise on either of these subjects would necessarily include the other. The Secret Doctrine is the oomplete Philosophy of Masonic Symbolism. So long as this philosophy is unknown to the Mason, his symbols are, to a great extent, dead letters, the work of the lodge a dumb show beyond its moral precepts, and the Genius of Masonry for the members of the Craft is largely the spirit of self-interest, mutual support, and physical enjoyment or revelry, the latest embodiment of which is the "Mystic Shrine." But there are some among the members of the Craft — and how many time alone can determine — who believe that Masonry means far more than this, and who have already discerned in its symbols and traditions something of their real meaning. Many of these have found partial clues which served to keep interest alive while searching for plainer meanings and deeper revelations. In retracing the steps by which these ancient symbols and their profound philosophy have come down to our own time, more and more obscured with every passing century, students have gathered a large number of facts, a great mass of traditions and general information, all of which have been variously interpreted by different writers on Masonry. All writers, however, agree in the conclusion that the symbols and traditions of Freemasonry come from the far East, and go back to the remotest antiquity.

So that the saying that the Mason journeys from West to East in search of light is literally true. This search is not one incited by curious interest only. If Masonry possesses merely a mass of curious myths and meaningless symbols, of what real value is it to any one to trace them down? What real benefit can it be to any one to demonstrate that five or ten thousand years ago the same curious myths) and meaningless symbols existed in the Mysteries of

Egypt, or were taught by Pythagoras and the followers of Zoroaster? Such, however, is not the genius of Freemasonry.

The real secrets of Masonry lie concealed in its Symbols, and these, constituting as they do a Picture Language, or Art Speech, are made to carry a complete philosophy of the existence and relations of Deity, Nature, and Man. The average Mason, taking the symbols for the things symbolized, and knowing nothing of the profound philosophy upon which they rest, is incredulous that it ever existed, and so he treads the "burning sands" in search of a novel sensation or a new joke. As mere pastimes these jovial entertainments are neither better nor worse than many others. They represent one extreme into which the Ancient Wisdom has degenerated. Let every intelligent Mason reflect on the sublimity and sanctity of the ceremonies in some of the degrees, where the name of Deity is invoked, where the highest moral precepts are inculcated, and where the purest and most exalted ethics are taught, and then let him ask himself the question, whether it is consistent and devoid of hypocrisy to round all this with a roaring farce? Does not such a course tend to make all sacred things also a mere matter of form, a jest and a byword?

Every Mason is familiar with this extreme and with the extent to which these recent innovations and associations have been carried, and the present writer is by no means the first to protest against it, however ungraciously his protest may be received or unpopular this work may be. Let every intelligent Mason admit, merely for the sake of the argument, that there is another extreme. Suppose it to be true and easily demonstrable, that the Symbols of Masonry embody and were originally designed to convey the most profound Wisdom, and that these symbols stand unchanged through all the ages, and are the means by which that wisdom may at any time be recovered by him who can find their true meaning. Masonry is, in a special sense, the custodian of these symbols, and it is its most common tradition that these and the Ancient Landmarks are to be preserved unaltered. This is the plainest and most logical deduction from the whole spirit of Masonry. These custodians are, in the highest degrees, called Princes of the Royal Secret — Nay, *Sublime* Princes of the Royal Secret! What a farce, what pretense, if there is no Royal Secret. Reflect a moment, good reader, and; especially good Brother Mason. What is the most sacred treasure, the most lasting possession of man? Is it not knowledge? Suppose a tidal wave should sweep all our seaports on the Eastern and Western coasts, and that this should be followed by cyclone and earthquake, so that the whole country should be completely devastated in a month. A few millions of our people remaining, with all our resources of knowledge, it might take half a century to recover a greater part of our prosperity. But suppose our people were all swept away, like many an ancient Civilization or Lost Empire; or suppose that all else remained, and we lost our store of knowledge, all Arts, all Sciences, and that our whole people were reduced to the condition of our North American Indians; half a century, then, would destroy all we have so laboriously wrought out, and we might pitch our wigwams in weed-grown streets, or amid crumbling ruins. What we have imagined of our own is but the history of other civilizations. The howling wastes of Gobi conceal, we are told, the remains of a civilization for outranking our own, and beneath the ocean's bed lie entombed the records and the monuments of man. Our most lasting possession is knowledge; and when this is swept away, desolation only remains. Bro. Pike says that the real secrets of Masonry, the philosophy concealed in its Symbols, are far older than the Vedas, and are at least ten thousand years old, and that the Art-Speech, which Symbolism is, was designed by real Princes of the Royal Secret, by Prince Adepts, or Perfect Masters, to conceal, preserve, and convey this Ancient Wisdom to the latest generations of men: That when Civilizations decayed, when Empires ceased to be, and when desolation brooded in silence over a whole continent, a "Rock beside the Water," or a symbol transplanted to another land might serve to convey the lost secret to another people and time. Knowing the course of Empire and the inevitable destiny of Races of man, these Sublime Princes of the Royal Secret, by wise forethought, determined that nothing should be lost. Such is the heritage of Masonry, and Bro. Pike proves this beyond all controversy by excerpts from the sacred books of all Religions, and by the most learned and painstaking investigation. The value of such investigations does not consist in proving the great antiquity of the Symbols of Freemasonry, for this is an easy task, and no one with the slightest knowledge of the subject dare dispute it, for the symbols are found on the oldest monuments, and described in the oldest records known to man. A far more difficult undertaking, the results of which are beyond all else valuable, is the effort to determine exactly what these symbols mean. If they were the precipitated results of profound knowledge, the very fruitage of all past civilizations, some of which transcended all we have yet achieved in the West, then to correctly interpret them, means the recovery of all past knowledge, in substance, if not in detail. This is precisely the interpretation and the value that should be put upon such results. This result is the recovery of the Lost Word of the Master, and the Symbol of that Word is the A. U. M. of the Persian Magi and the most Ancient Brahman, because, back of that tri-literal glyph lies the Philosophy of the Secret Doctrine, the Synthesis of all Knowledge. Let any Prince of the Royal Secret examine the evidence and judge for himself. If, instead of doing this, he prefers to sneer at these statements, and to ridicule the whole subject, while he still boasts the title of Prince Adept, he stands as three men once stood near the coast of Joppa, self-convicted by the imprecations of his own mouth. The present revival of Philosophy in the West ought to bring about the restoration of this old wisdom. While it cannot interfere with the Masonic organization in the least, or seek to reveal any of its ceremonies, grips, or passwords, by which the secrets of Masonry may be obtained unlawfully, it must give the largest credit to the fidelity with which the Symbols and Ancient Landmarks have been preserved by the organization of Freemasons, and seek the co-operation of all earnest and true Masons in the recovery of the Lost Word, and in promulgating this sublime philosophy for the benefit of the whole human race.

There is an old occult maxim which declares that "Nothing is concealed from him who knows." No Mason is bound to conceal that which he has never learned in the Lodge. All else he receives as he learns anything, places his own estimate upon its value, and becomes individually responsible for its use. It must be a matter of conscience, and be weighed in the balance of duty, and everyone must abide by the result. If Masonry has lost the Royal Secret, or if it never possessed it, or if it was wrenched away in the very name of Religion little more than a century ago, all the same, it belongs to the Craft as the Heir-apparent of the Old Wisdom. But the time has come when no cable-tow can bind it. It now belongs to Humanity equally with the Mason. To this end has it been preserved throughout the centuries.

What a future lies before Masonry should it determine to enter into its birthright to possess it. Thoroughly organized as it is, and counting its membership by tens of thousands, rehabilitated in its ancient wisdom, it may become an irresistible force in shaping the present civilization, and in influencing the future destiny of Man. All else has perished from the civilizations of the past. Wisdom alone is immortal of all the possessions of man. Of all the achievements of Classic Greece nothing is so well remembered today as the school of Pythagoras, and the Philosophy of Plato, and these but embody and were founded upon the Royal Secret of every Prince Adept Mason. To restore the Royal Secret would be a work, which, when completed, would be to our present humanity what the supporting Columns are to the Lodge: Wisdom, Strength and Beauty. (Knowledge, Power and Harmony.) It would introduce new methods, and motives, and new ideals into modern education, and give us in a few generations other Platos. If we create the conditions the results are sure to follow. Here lies the reward for all the trials and persecutions to which Masons have been subjected in the past. Here we may build the monument of all its Heroes and Martyrs. We may so build that seeing it they would rejoice that they suffered to the end. Bacon dreamed of a great "Instauration," a recovery of knowledge, and possession of wisdom from Inductive Philosophy alone; but on such lines it must be forever a dream. The old Philosophy is both inductive and deductive, through the perfect equilibrium of Reason and Intuition, or Experience and Aspiration, and is scientific to the last degree. It will give us as a result Knowledge and Power without oppression; Religion without superstition; Universal Liberty, Toleration and Fraternity; Universal Compassion; Peace on Earth, and Good-will to Man.

Of course it is in the province of Masonry to elect, if it chooses, that its symbols shall have only a superficial meaning in the Lodge. It may admit that it has adopted from the ancient mysteries the glyphs and parables that once served to embody and convey the most complete and profound philosophy, and, while adopting these symbols and the ancient art-speech, confine their use and interpretation to such lessons of equity, morality, and fraternity, as are to be found in all exoteric religions.

The author of this book would be the last to ignore or to belittle the value of ethical or moral precepts. But these are the basis of conduct, not the crown of existence; the beginning, not the end if wisdom.

Man's "general infancy," as Browning puts it, only begins when his code of ethics is complete, and when he is perfected as man. To spend the greater part of his days in transgression and repentance is not Man's "object served, his end Attained, his genuine strength put fairly forth."

Masonry not only nowhere denies this deeper meaning to its symbolism, but many writers have admitted it and expatiated upon it, but very few seem to have been able to discern the real meaning. They have generally failed because of sectarian bias, which dwarfed their vision and narrowed the ancient Wisdom Religion to the bounds of a modern creed, while the genius of the ancient wisdom is universal and all-inclusive. To deny or to ignore any but the most superficial view is to adopt such conclusions as those arrived at by the Astronomer Royal of Scotland, who makes of the Coffer in the King's chamber of the great pyramid of Ghezeh, only "a corn-bin!" It is to profane the holy vessels, and at last to materialize all spiritual things. It may justly be doubted whether any man for the past century and a half has done so much toward restoring Masonry to its birthright as Grand Master Albert Pike. His writings are a mine of wealth too little known to the great majority of Masons. The recent Jesuitical attack on his memory is not only a palpable and sensational lie, but it should serve to arouse every Prince of the Royal Secret to a deeper knowledge of the value of Bro. Pike's work. That work not only abounds in the clearest exposition of all the Masonic virtues, and reveals a mind incapable of baseness, but, passing beyond these to the full stature of Manhood, grasps those eternal principles which underlie the building of Cosmos and the evolution and regeneration of man. The charge that such a man, breathing reverence to truth, love to man, and aspiration toward light in every sentence of his voluminous writings, could descend to bestiality and grovel in convulsions at the feet of a confessed devil-worshiper, is worthy of his real accusers; and yet such is the voluminous attack recently made in the pages of a leading New York daily. The attack but thinly veils the old-time assassins of the heroes and martyrs of Masonry, and is designed to frighten the ignorant and superstitious into fresh hatred of Masonry. This hysterical "Granddaughter of Astarte" is herself a victim, if she has any real existence at all, of the same nefast body, and is only a fit subject for a madhouse. History repeats itself; and this fresh attack upon Masonry, while it can not tarnish the fame of the honored dead, should warn Masons that even in this enlightened age the minions of the Prince of Darkness and the Father of Lies have not renounced their allegiance or forgotten their cunning. Persecution is to the Truth what the winds and the rains are to the sprouting oak. These but sink deeper the roots of conviction, and spread wider the leaves that are for the healing of the Nations. If Masons will but pass from refreshment to labor and unite in rebuilding the City and Temple of the Lord of Truth, recover the Lost Word, and rehabilitate the ancient Wisdom, she may paraphrase the saying of Macaulay in his essay on Barere, and apply it to all her enemies: "We therefore like his invectives against us much better than anything else he has written...It was but little that he could do to promote the honor of our country; but that little he did strenuously and constantly. Renegade, traitor, slave, coward, liar, slanderer, murderer, hack-writer, police-spy — the one small service which he could render to England was to hate her; and such as he was may all who hate her be." Masonry need not fear the hatred of such, and only such will hate her if she enters into her priceless inheritance, bears aloft her banners and emblazons with light her time-honored Landmarks.

SO MOTE IT BE.

Postscript to the Fifth Edition

The original *thesis* of "*Mystic Masonry*" may be defined as follows:

To show and illustrate the profound wisdom embodied in the philosophy that underlies and runs like a golden thread throughout the whole Institution of Freemasonry: To demonstrate through this philosophy and its use, illustrations, dramatic representations and symbolism, that the "Work of the Lodge" constitutes a *Great School of Instruction* for its candidates and Fraters, in the real meaning of life, and the basic principles of human conduct, so as to secure the highest and most noble results ever revealed to man: To render absurd and illogical any other inference from the references to, and all that we know of, the real Masters of the past, and the Schools, and the "Greater Mysteries" of antiquity.

Masonry seems to have embodied, crystallized, preserved and adapted to the present age, these Jewels of all the past, divested of all extraneous or irrelevant matters.

This is the meaning of the *Perfect Ashlar.* The author was well aware that but few Masons realized what a treasure-house of Jewels they possessed, and that some, perhaps, would regard such a claim as absurd, and altogether fanciful.

He was also aware that there are thousands of Brother Masons who believe that there must be far deeper truths, and more valuable treasures, concealed, than are revealed, or generally apprehended, if they only knew where to search, and how to discover them; for he has heard this statement oft-repeated by Brothers, young and old.

Indeed, it is difficult to imagine how any intelligent and thoughtful man can go through the dramatic and monitorial Initiation of the three degrees of the Blue Lodge, and come to any other conclusion.

To justify this logical inference, encourage the intelligent search for the Royal ' Secret, and assist in the Recovery of the Lost Word was the original and only motive of *"Mystic Masonry."*

The author has been a Mason nearly half a century and aside from the study of Masonry, its sources, symbolism and essential meaning, has been able to check and verify these great truths from another source, viz., the study of man, and especially from the study of Psychology. Here the opportunities to test theories of life, and the motives of conduct and elements of character really transcend all others.

The physician sees like none other, both the beginning and the end of embodied human life. From the "first breath", often so anxiously looked for and evoked, of the little one, that

"Out from the shore of the Great Unknown,
Comes weeping and wailing, and all alone" —

to the last breath of the aged just crossing the Great Divide, the physician is present, often nearer than any other, and vigilant, observing, solicitous, and full of deep reflection. It is his office to try to understand, in order that he may apply and utilize then, and thereafter.

It may seem to some a startling and unwarranted statement, that the most profound truths of Psychology, [the building of Character, and self-control which more than all else safeguards against disease, paresis, premature senility and insanity,] are all embodied in the very foundations of Freemasonry. But this is the simple truth. To illustrate and verify here would be out of place, but it is a thesis easily demonstrated. Masonry embodies a Science of Ethics, of human conduct and character, found scarcely anywhere else; and more than half of all our diseases come from lack of self-control and from selfish indulgence.

Every Mason knows, and I am writing principally for Brother Masons, that this government, of which, in spite of all its faults, we are so justly proud, was inspired and founded mostly by men who were Masons. The "truths" that were "self-evident", and the "rights" that were "inalienable", were perceived in and by those founders as derived from Masonry. They were transplanted directly from Masonry to the "Declaration", and the "Constitution", though we have not yet altogether realized them. This is why Albert Pike and others have called Masonry the "Great Republic".

They tried to define the *Eminent Domain,* the "Reserved Right" of every Individual, every Citizen, to Life, Liberty and the pursuit of Happiness. These Inalienable Rights were founded on "Self-evident Truths".

Before a candidate takes the slightest obligation in Masonry, and as the premise of every obligation taken, he is given the *unqualified assurance* that *no obligation required of him* shall interfere with any duty he owes to God, to his Country, to his neighbor, or himself; and he alone is to be the Judge of these duties. These are his "Inalienable Rights"; his "recognized Duties; his

Eminent Domain. Enlarged and elaborated, defined and codified, here is our "Declaration of Independence", our "Constitution of a Free People", and it is the Genius of Freemasonry pure and simple. It is impossible to enslave either the body, mind or soul of man while these principles and declarations are strictly and logically adhered to. Nor were the founders of this Government "Of the People, by the People, for the People" either in ignorance or in doubt as to the danger point, for they proceeded to *forever separate Church and State,* as far as possible. The Government was to be a *State* affair, with which the Church had, *officially,* nothing to do whatsoever.

Rome declares in America today, that Church and State shall be united as *one;* and that *one* shall be *the Church.* I hereby challenge every Freemason in America today to *Take Notice* of this Sign and Summons.

To the profound Philosophy of Life, and the stores of Ancient Wisdom to which it was the original design of this little book to call attention, there is now added an imminent duty of Citizenship, for which the Freemason ought to be better prepared and more strongly obligated than any other, for the simple reason that these duties and obligations are taught, ingrained, and illustrated in the School of Masonry, specifically and concisely as no where else in the world today.

This is why Rome hates, vilifies and anathematizes Masonry continually, relentlessly and eternally. There can be no compromise. Shall it be Church, or State, to rule in this "Free Country"? It cannot possibly be both. Rome today is the most powerful and ambitious *Political Autocracy* on earth, and she already holds the *Balance of Power* in America!

I have said nothing here of the Religious department of the Roman Hierarchy. That is "another story".

The Mason who is untrue to the basic principles of Masonry, can be nothing less than a Traitor to his Country. There can be no middle ground, no compromise.

If the more than two million Masons in the United States today, would *do their duty,* as did that handful of men and Masons who signed our Declaration of Independence, we should have a bloodless revolution, and the Italian Cardinals who run the Politics of the Roman Church would "*get out of politics*", so far as America is concerned; while the Catholic *religion* would have the same rights and benefits here as any other; no more, no less.

Of what value or use is the Wisdom of the Ages if we fail to put its principles in practice, or to utilize its profound lessons running through the whole history of man?

Every just and Upright Mason ought to know and to realize what he stands for, why he is a Mason, and that while his freedom is reserved, his "inalienable rights" were secured by sacrifice, and can only be preserved by conscientious *regard and discharge of duty.*

"Eternal vigilance is the price of Liberty". The greatest enemy of the Republic today is the man who stupidly or indifferently says, "There is no danger". This is the strongest asset of the enemy of all our Liberties. Get a word of this danger into any influential newspaper if you can. They are all "censored".

"Mother Church" and "The Party" are *political* slogans, pure and simple; built for "graft", and founded on greed, equally unscrupulous and menacing.

I have not a particle of fear that any intelligent, just and upright Mason will deny, or be able to disprove a single statement herein made. The facts are scarcely outlined. The fear and the danger are that Masons will continue to ignore, belittle or evade them.

The present point of attack is our Free Public Schools, the very foundation of all our Free Institutions; and the Parochial Schools are fast gaining ground.

The most hopeful sign is the Resolution recently passed by the National Teachers Association, unanimously protesting *against any division of the School fund, for any Sectarian body whatsoever.*

Nothing is easier than to demonstrate that the Principles which Masonry so clearly defines and upon which the Lodge is built, constitute the *Magna Charta* of this Government, and were thence derived. These principles are the pure gold of ethics and the conduct of life, both individual and associate, from the melting pot of all human history, and the wisdom of all ages.

This is why "Mother Church", that is, the sixty-odd Italian Cardinals, arrogant, ambitious, relentless, vindictive, hate Masonry, misrepresent it, and continually anathematize it, and would destroy it if they could, as they have murdered its votaries in the past.

Masonry stands squarely across their path; stands for the exact opposite of all their political ambition covets and would gain at any cost to mankind; for with them, "the end justifies the means".

Not one citizen in a thousand realizes what immense progress this Political Autocracy has made in America in the fourteen years since this little book was written.

In Canada today the citizens are trying to undo the work of Popery and Jesuitism in the Public Schools, shake off the blight of Priestcraft and regain their Liberties. Read the Canadian papers and see, for they are not all censored.

Of what value is a knowledge of history if we are never to profit by its bitter lessons and admonitions? Of what value is a knowledge of the basic principles that underlie all individual and social life, if we are not ready to utilize them, live by them, and, if need be, fight for them and die for them, as did the Fathers of this Republic?

I can only speak and act as one man, already entered on his "fourth score" of years, and a Mason for nearly fifty years. In many countries today, I would pay the forfeit of life, for these utterances; and in this country six deliberate attempts within the year have been made to assassinate one of my Masonic Comrades engaged in the same cause.

So far as publicity and our open "Declaration" are concerned in this country, we have not yet made a beginning. But so far as the enemy of all our Free Institutions is concerned, scarcely a department of our Government, or one of our Safeguards of Freedom exists that is not by them already undermined. Free School, Free Press, Free Religion — all undermined by Jesuitry, and paying tribute to Rome!

During the past fourteen years I have advanced from the reflections of philosophy, to the "Church Militant", as every just and upright Mason will, ere long, be compelled to pass from "refreshment to labor", or become a traitor to every Masonic principle, and implicated in the destruction of every design on his trestleboard.

In *"Mystic Masonry"* I have tried to give a glimpse of the Jewels of Wisdom, the Crown Jewels of every high civilization that has ever existed, inspired by their sages and wisest Masters.

Year by year my convictions have deepened, the glory and beauty become more and more transcendent, and the outlook more uplifting on the Journey of Life.

Scarcely a proposition herein contained, drawn from Philosophy and Symbolism, and justified by analogy and rational sequence, that has not since been confirmed by Natural Science, and reaffirmed by the author of *"The Great Work"*.

I undertook consistently to portray the qualifications that should constitute a "Master", such as I had not seen or known. A score of times I said to the Beloved Comrade, "I am waiting for the *Man*", and one day I found him.

I find no incongruity between the logical inference I had drawn and the actuality I had discovered. It was like pointing a telescope at the nidus of perturbations in space, and locating a new planet.

The whole of Masonry, the sequence of symbolism, pointed in this one direction, led to no other inference, would have added q.e.d. to no other solution of the problem. For seven years I have been making careful observations of the orbit and movements of the new star on my horizon, and been rewarded by assurance, confirmation, satisfaction and higher aspiration.

Good men and women seem so often discouraged and bewildered over the experiences of life. To the everlasting question, "What does it all mean?" often comes the discouraged, and discouraging answer, "Nobody knows".

How to adjust the vicissitudes of life, and to utilize its varying experiences, so as to become *Master of the results upon ourselves,* that is the Royal Secret, the Great Work.

Facing, as we must, Principalities and Powers, things present, and things to come, and Life and Death, and yet to remain serene, steadfast, and full of good cheer, is the Great Secret. Does this not imply a mental attitude — a way of -looking at things — a method of living — an assurance that we are on the right path — and a conviction that *all is well,* and the goal secure?

Masonry is a Great School, designed and qualified to educate every initiate in just this Science of Life. What else is the meaning of the "Instructive Tongue, the Listening Ear and the Faithful Breast"? What else can it be to be "made a Mason *in the heart*"? Is not that an expression of *reality* and *sincerity*? What else can the expression — "By being a *Man*", mean? Certainly not a coward, a slave, a fanatic, or an imbecile. Test the noblest characters of all time by these principles and these standards and see if they are not revealed.

This is the Great School of Masonry coming down through the ages, whether one student in a thousand *Graduates,* and "makes good", or not.

The "Infallible" Pope says we are "Atheists", and do not believe in God. *He knows better.* No man can pass to the Altar of Masonry who does not believe in God, as two million American Masons will testify.

Freemasonry is aligned with Eternal Truth, Liberty, Charity and Fraternity, and it lies squarely across the pathway of all who would enslave the human soul, and there it will stand so long as God is in the Heavens, and till Time shall be no more.

Murder, as Rome has often tried to do, every Freemason on earth today, and not one of its principles, its Priceless Jewels would be changed or lost. You might as well try to destroy the principles of Light, Electricity or Gravitation.

One of the *relics* preserved for pious Catholics in the East, we are told, is a bottle containing "the darkness that fell upon Egypt". If his "Infallible Holiness" should look upon this bottle he would undoubtedly behold his own image reflected there, with his swarm of Italian Cardinals hovering like locusts in the background and his "bottle of darkness" would indeed prove a *boomerang.*

What Egypt *was* in its glory, when the Great Masters instituted its Paternal Government, and built the "Rock beside the Waters", America may yet become if every Mason is true to his Landmarks and his traditions, and to the Fathers who instituted them here.

What Egypt *is today,* America will become, a waste of sand and howling jackals, if the same Priestcraft and Paganism that triumphed there, are allowed here to destroy our Free Schools, and *reunite* Church and State.

The issues are exceedingly plain, and as old as the human race on this earth.

Since the "Lost Word" may be "discovered" in the "Great Work", the designs upon the trestleboard are restored for the first time in many a weary century. Only the Listening Ear, and the Faithful Breast are required. I, for one, have *listened,* examined the Jewel, and found the Mark.

Fraternally,

J. D. Buck.

Cincinnati, June 1911.

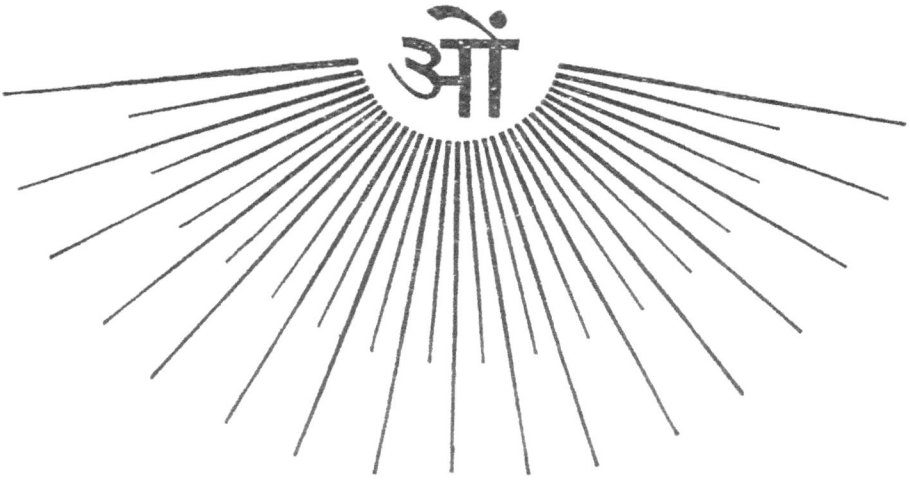

"Unveil — O thou that giveth sustenance to the universe, from whom all things proceed, to whom all must return, — that face of the true Sun now hidden by a vase of Golden Light, that we may know the truth, and do our whole duty on our journey to thy sacred seat."

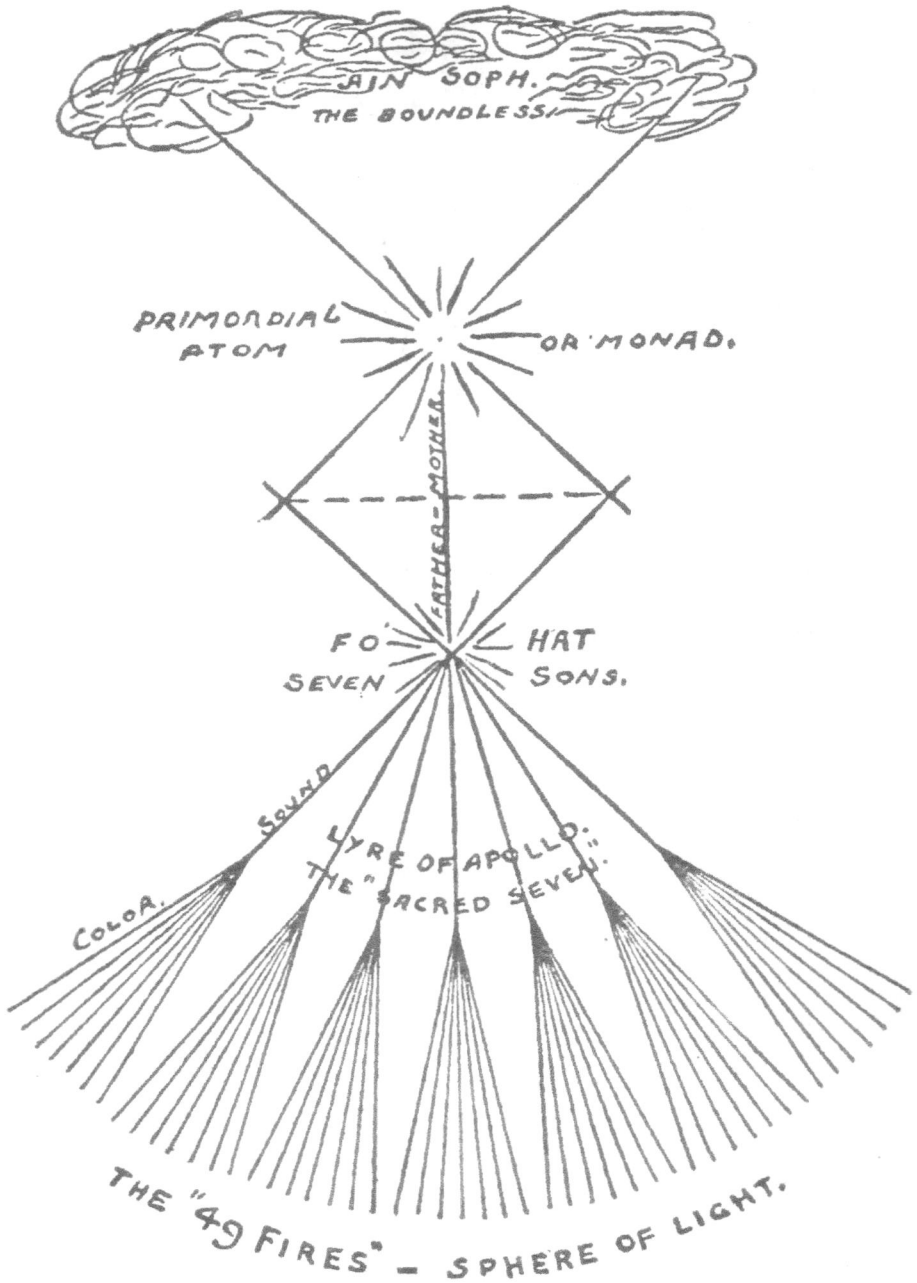

Plate I.

Descent of Spirit into Matter.
"All Things From One."

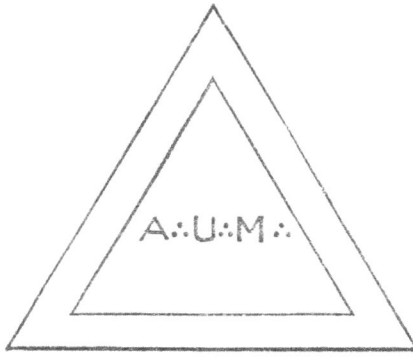

Plate II.

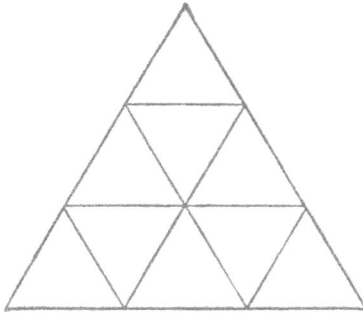

Plate III.
The First Differentiation.

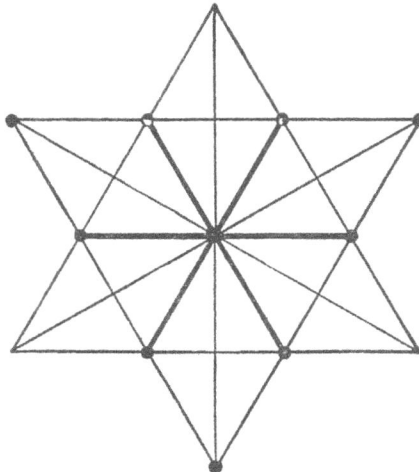

Plate IV.
The Second Differentiation.

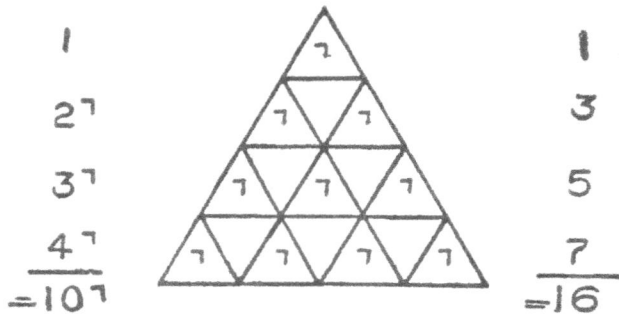

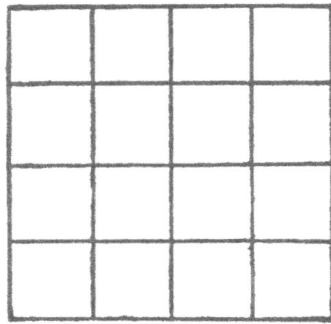

1
2
3
4
―
=10

1
3
5
7
―
=16

4
4
4
4
―
=16

Plate V.
Tetragrammaton of Pythagoras.

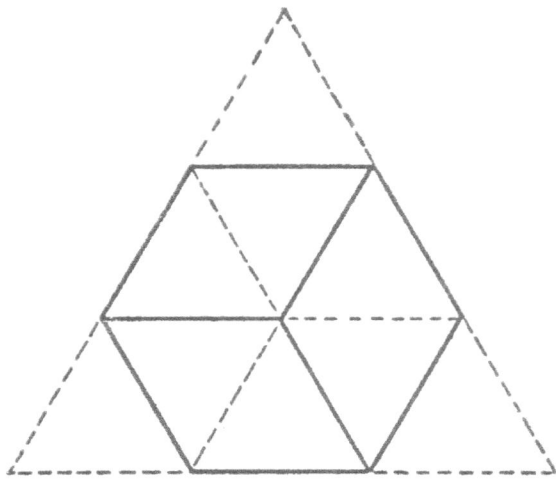

Plate VI.
The Relation of Spirit to Matter.

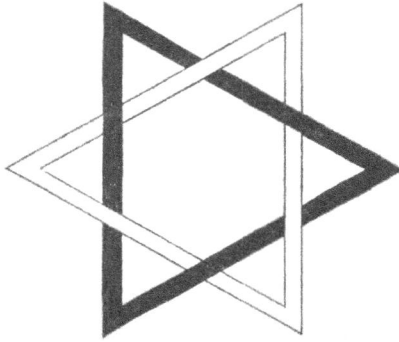

Plate VII.
Matter and Spirit in Equilibrium.

Plate VIII.
The Greater Tetraktys.

"I praise Thee with my Lips,
I know not the numbers."

Plate IX.
"The Stone that the Builders rejected."

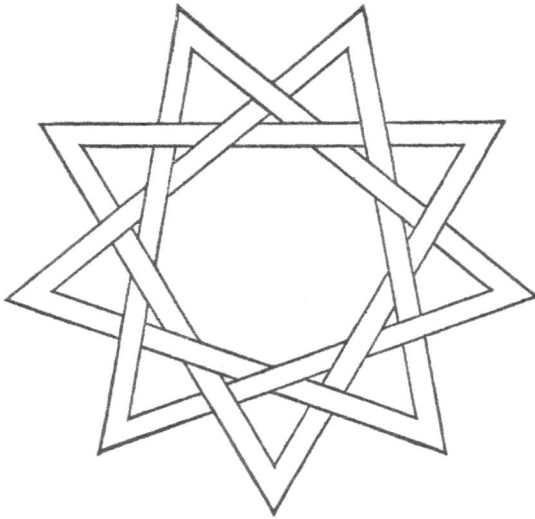

Plate X.
Trinity of Trinities.

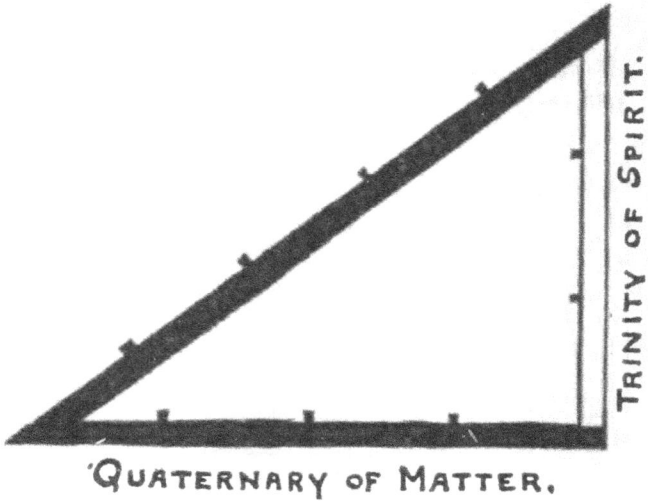

Plate XI.
The "Forty Seventh Problem" — Diversity in Unity.

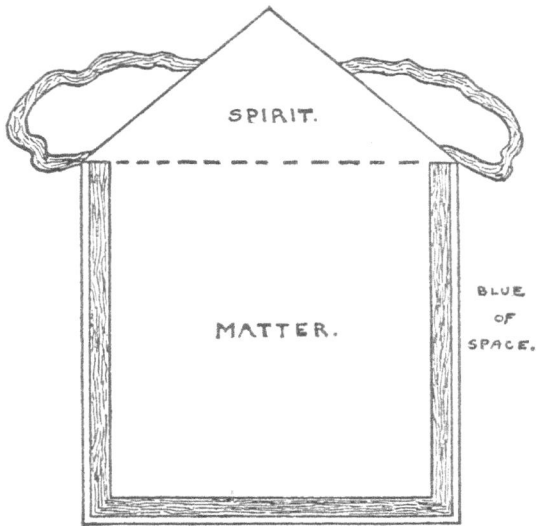

SPIRIT.

MATTER.

BLUE OF SPACE.

Plate XII.
The Lamb-skin, or White Apron.

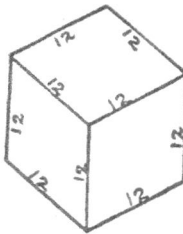

12 12 12 12 12 12 12 12 12

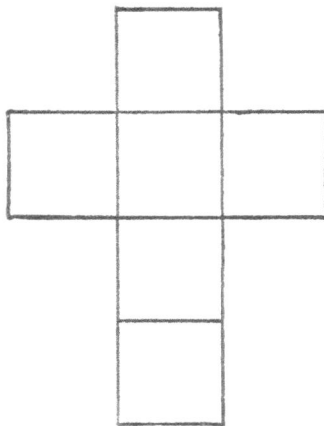

Plate XIII.
The Cube Unfolded.

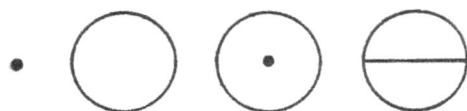

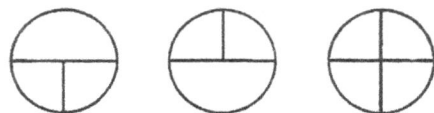

Plate XIV.
The Sequence of Symbols &c.

www.ingramcontent.com/pod-product-compliance
Lightning Source LLC
Chambersburg PA
CBHW030023290326
41934CB00005B/458